The Conservative Vampire

MR. EVIL

DEDICATION

This book is dedicated to my wife, Mrs. Evil, who is also my editor, spell-checker, inspiration, prime Rummikub opponent, and partner-in-crime. I could not be Mr. Evil without her.

CONTENTS

Acknowledgments   i

Introduction   1

The Conservative Vampire   6

"Forgive Me, Pastor, But My Heroes Have Always Been Cowboys..."   10

There's A Reason For the Fireworks   15

They Deserve It, But...   17

A Cold-Hearted Republican   20

OZ: An Interesting Place to Visit   23

My Wife's Calendar   27

Welcome to My Hate Filled Home   30

It's A Mad Mad Mad Mad World   34

Married With Children   38

Where Have All the Conservatives Gone?   42

My Great Great Great Great Great Grandfather Says He's Sorry. But He Doesn't Mean It Because He's Dead!!! — 44

The Return of Judas — 46

How To Know When A Republican is in the Room — 49

What You Win Prizes For in Europe — 52

A Matter of Trust — 55

Why Refugees Keep Coming — 60

My Psychic Wife — 63

Trump VS. Jesus — 66

How Can You Make TV Commercials Even Worse — 78

A Modest Proposal For Ending Gun Violence and Saving the Second Amendment — 82

Let's Call The Mueller Hearing What They Were: Elder Abuse — 86

A Skunk By Any Other Name — 89

Equality — 92

The First Amendment Is Dead In New York City — 95

Amazing Predictions For 2020 — 98

The Art of A Wink And The Deal — 103

"She" is Worth Fighting For! — 109

A Really Inconvenient Truth — 112

When Green Is Actually Red — 114

A New Word For Liberals — 118

Odds And Ends You Missed In The News — 121

Go, Coach Joe! — 124

Can Notre Dame Be Saved From Architects, Politicians, and Political Correctness? — 127

Final Thoughts From A Conservative Vampire — 131

Appendix — 137

ACKNOWLEDGMENTS

Books like this are not written without an exchange of ideas, many thoughtful discussions, and inspirations of enormous value. I acknowledge my few conservative friends, whom I will not name for privacy reasons, who have inspired me with their traditional thoughts and values. They keep my wife and me sane. You know who you are.

I also acknowledge the fine journalists at Fox News, who prove that journalism is not quite dead.

INTRODUCTION

I am evil – pure evil. I am proud of my evil nature, proud of the thoughts that make me evil, proud of my evil actions and delighted in my proclivity to choose the darkest path.

Yes, I am human like the rest of you. Not a devil, demon or wicked beast out of horror fantasies. A real human, mortal, someone you might pass by on the street or sit next to on a plane.

I possess no magical powers or extraordinary ability to control the minds or movements of those around me. Yet, I assure you, I am evil!

Since we as people don't always see the truth about ourselves, how do I know this?

First, my children, now young adults, have explained it to me. Additionally, my friends, neighbors and acquaintances have seen through my soul. They have admonished and shamed me for my actions, comments, thoughts, and my very existence. Some of them negate me and pretend that I don't exist. Others threaten me with violence. All of these are the wages of my evil nature.

Now that you know that I'm evil, what makes me so?

I have discovered that I was born that way. Born a white male and unwilling to apologize for it.

I'm a racist because I believe that the United States should have secure borders and a coherent immigration policy. Two hundred years ago, some of my ancestors were slave owners, but I feel no obligation to apologize because I did not know them, nor did I have any control over their actions or beliefs.

I'm stupid and uninformed because I believe that all life is sacred and a gift from God, born and unborn.

I love my country and unabashedly believe that it is the greatest in the world. I refuse to ask for forgiveness for believing in the Constitution of the United States and standing at attention for the American flag and the national anthem.

I believe that my actions have consequences and that I am responsible for my decisions, my activities, and my impact on the world.

I want to pay my fair share of taxes, but I'm better qualified than the government to determine how the bulk of my wealth is spent.

I'm a potential lunatic and mass murderer because I own guns and believe in a constitutional right to carry them.

I'm someone who should be silenced because of my unreasonable views and my belief in free speech.

In general, at one time, my values were typical American values. Now, they're "extremist" and "dangerous." In short, they're "evil."

I am a retired college administrator, an internationally recognized fine art photographer, a writer and blogger.

About a year ago, I started publishing a conservative blog: ConservativesAreEvil.com. I write and produce this blog anonymously, not because I'm ashamed of what I say or who I am – but because my wife insists. She is afraid for me and our family. She is afraid of physical violence or harm that might come our way because of my viewpoints, which she largely agrees with. She is afraid of being ostracized by our "friends" and acquaintances. She is afraid of ruining the future careers of our children. She is afraid of many things, all of which come from being known as a conservative. Therefore, I adopted the pseudonym: Mr. Evil.

My website was inspired by a quote from the late Dr. Charles Krauthammer:

"To understand the workings of American politics, you have to understand this fundamental law: Conservatives think liberals are stupid. Liberals think conservatives are evil."

It is important to note that my website and the opinions expressed within are my own work and are not produced or endorsed by Dr. Krauthammer or anyone associated with him. Unfortunately, Dr. Krauthammer passed away before this site came into existence.

ConservativesAreEvil.com is produced by me as an individual. It is not paid for by a big company or corporation. It reflects my personal thoughts and opinions – right or wrong.

The essays in this book originated in my blog and appear here with only minor editing. In each article, I start off with a short introduction to give you background on why I originally wrote the essay. In some cases, it is necessary to cite the news event or activity that prompted me to write the entry.

The title of this book, *The Conservative Vampire* was also the first article I wrote for my blog. And it is the first chapter in this book.

In several of the articles, I make references to TV shows, movies, or other items of popular culture. I have included a short appendix in the back of this book in which those references are explained and/or credited. After all, not everyone knows who

Kolchak is. If you do, congratulations! The appendix also lists URL links to websites or online articles I refer to in the essays.

If you are a conservative, you will probably agree with many of the points of view I take. My articles may arm you with bits of knowledge to act as ammunition when trying to persuade others of your conservative viewpoints. However, if you are a liberal, progressive, socialist, moderate, or whatever other label, I urge you to read this manuscript thoughtfully and deliberately, not that it will change your mind, but it may help you to know the other side. You may finally understand why "conservatives are evil" and what makes them so.

This is the very first essay to appear in my blog. From February of 2019, it is a commentary on the "conservatives are evil" theme.

THE CONSERVATIVE VAMPIRE

Imagine that you know the truth: vampires are real! Just like in the movies, they're evil, bloodsucking creatures of the night. Given the opportunity, they will destroy you, your family, your neighborhood.

Now imagine that you know for a fact that the neighbor who just moved into the big house on the hill is a real vampire. You've called the police and all the authorities, but they think you're a nut. And to top it off, Roddy McDowall isn't available to offer his cinematic vampire-hunter advice. Darren

McGavin is busy tracking down a golum, so you're on your own.

What do you do?

Do you allow this creature to exist in your neighborhood? Do you drive it out? Do you go over in friendship with a six-pack of hard lemonade and try to reason with the creature?

You've seen the movies! You know the answer! You must sneak in and drive a stake through its hideous heart!

You did the right thing, you know you did!

Now, let's imagine a slight change of scenario. We'll change only one word. "Vampire" now becomes "Conservative."

You're a good progressive liberal with enough knowledge to know that this conservative who just moved in is evil, a danger to all.

This is real life, so unlike in the vampire movies, you can't just barge in with a wooden spike and dispatch him with the same relish Hillary displayed when wiping her email server clean with a lint-free cloth. Instead, you must let him know he's not wanted. Maybe you let the air out of his tires, or splash some paint over his "I Heart Trump" bumper sticker. Or even worse, you plaster his car with "I Feel the Bern" stickers! You turn your head and ignore him when you pass him on the street. You don't invite him to social functions, and you would never attend a party where you knew he might be in attendance. You tell all your family and neighbors about him, so they, too, can join you in making him feel unwelcome. If you hear that he's going to make a speech at the local school or college, you lead a protest because his views are dangerous.

Believe it or not, we changed only one word and turned a fiction horror story into today's reality.

If you're liberal, you probably believe that conservatives are evil and you respond accordingly.

If you're conservative, you know that what I'm saying is true. Many of us won't put a Trump sticker on our car because we know it will be vandalized and make us a target for ridicule from the neighbors. We invite "friends" over, but don't discuss politics because they will be out the door before finishing their first dry martinis.

My wife and I attended one of the ubiquitous Trump rallies a few months back. Every time television cameras came near, she turned her back to them because she didn't want her co-workers to see her, as it would have been disastrous for her career and social life. Her hair dresser who was also there did the same thing, saying she would lose most of her clients if they knew she attended a Trump rally. I ran into an old colleague. Before I even said "hi," he started explaining: "You know, I just came out to see the crowd. I'm not into politics, you know. It was just something to do on a slow Saturday blah blah blah..."

It's funny. You show up as a conservative in broad daylight, in the purifying rays of the sun, and liberals don't understand why you don't just shrivel up and die, frying like a strip of crispy bacon in a hot cast iron skillet.

It's tough to be a vampire, er, I mean conservative.

I am of the age that when I was a young boy, kids still
played outside. Our heroes were different from the
heroes kids have now. It's too bad that a certain liberal
pastor obviously never knew the joys of pretending to be
a cowboy. This is a true story.

"FORGIVE ME, PASTOR, BUT MY HEROES HAVE ALWAYS BEEN COWBOYS..."

*"I grew up a-dreamin' of bein' a cowboy
And lovin' the cowboy ways
Pursuin' the life of my high ridin' heroes
I burned up my childhood days..."*

-- Sharon Vaughn

Willie Nelson sang it in *The Electric Cowboy*. Sharon Vaughn wrote the song. And it speaks to me of the days when my brothers and I, along with neighborhood kids, became good guy cowboys and bad guy rustlers and outlaws. We were six or ten years old, all with hats, cap guns and holster belts. Our parents approved of our outside activities and the good guys always beat the bad guys. We were spending time away from the TV, but we always became the heroes we saw on TV and in the movies.

I still watch Gene Autry, Roy Roger, and Tex Ritter (the singing cowboy actor and father of John Ritter from *Three's Company* and *8 Simple Rules*). I also listen to old programs from the classic days of radio (on satellite radio) like *Hopalong Cassidy*, *Gunsmoke* (far superior to the TV version), and *The Cisco Kid.* Yes, those programs were from a very different time. Good guys were good guys. Bad guys were bad guys. There were few nuances. In the shows intended for children, the good guys would shoot the guns out of the hands of the bad guys. There was no blood.

Many men who grew up between the 1920's through the 1970's know what I'm talking about. No, it wasn't a girl thing, and if you were a girl and wanted to play with us, we wouldn't let you. Sorry, but that's how it was.

I'm also aware that not everyone was so fortunate as to be able to enjoy such an upbringing. While I'm sure that there was much crossover in other classes and cultures, the cowboy phenomenon was largely a white middle-class thing, and certainly almost all male.

Sorry, if I've bored you, because I'm sure much of my audience knows all of this.

But it brings me forward into the 21st Century, when the idea that you might buy your six-year-old a toy gun marks you as an unfit parent and someone who has little regard for life and safety.

One Sunday morning, my wife and I found ourselves in church, which is typical for a Sunday morning. Our minister that Sunday morning was a stand-in, but he often officiates when the regular minister isn't available. Time after time, in his sermon he has made disparaging remarks about this country, our military, our government and those who believe in traditional values. This time was the last straw, and the reason that I will never attend church again if he is present.

He is a black minister and grew up in the inner city, but nowhere near Chicago. Apparently, in his own eyes, this made him an expert on black-on-black violence in Chicago. I must admit, however, that he is a great orator with immense persuasive power.

"Someone asked me the other day, why we don't do something to stop black people from killing black people in Chicago," he said, fire in his eyes. "This man told me that something has to be done to stop the culture of killing, the total disregard for human life. We have to take extreme measures, this man told me."

The congregation looked on, holding on to every word.

"Let me tell you what I told him," the pastor said. "I told him that we've already taken extreme measures. We've taken extreme measures to teach all these young black men all they know about shooting other people, about being callous about human life. We've taught them it's fine to pull out a gun and laugh as you kill the man next to you. That's what we've taught them. And this didn't start just yesterday. Oh, no! It started a long time ago. It started with Roy Rogers, John Wayne, and Gene Autry: men who taught us that having a gun makes you right!"

He continued. "You may not remember it, but back in the day, you could take a thin dime and spend a whole day in a movie theater watching people kill each other with guns. That's the society WE created. So don't get on your high horse and tell me about the good old days when Hopalong Cassidy was righteous with his blazing six guns. Instead, think about these young black men in Chicago who don't know anything better because we taught them it was the right thing to do. It's all on us. It's not on them!

I was nauseated and sickened. But some of the congregation applauded.

With only a few words, the pastor had twisted the truth beyond recognition. My cowboy heroes who reluctantly used weapons only as a last resort were transformed into uncaring killers. The values they upheld: truth, honor, justice, compassion, and perseverance, no longer meant anything.

What amazed me most was that at the end of the sermon, the pastor offered no solution to the problem of blacks killing blacks in Chicago. There was only blame. And the blame fell on the "good guys" I had grown up with.

I think that most of my audience knows that few, if any, of those young black men who perpetrate violence on each other in Chicago know anything about Gene Autry, Roy Rogers, or the Cisco Kid. It's a shame because if they had been brought up with Dale and Roy and Trigger, along with the values they represent, their lives might be far better and there would be fewer people killing each other on the streets of Chicago.

Here's to my heroes, who have always been cowboys!

This is a very short essay that appeared in my blog on the 4th of July, 2019. Unfortunately, history is short-changed in school these days. But things don't just happen for no reason. Have you ever wondered why we have fireworks on Independence Day?

THERE'S A REASON FOR THE FIREWORKS

The *Declaration of Independence* is dated July 4th, 1776. Most people don't know that John Adams insisted that fireworks be a part of our national celebration of independence even before the signing of the document. On the night of July 4, 1777, one year after the great document became a part of history, America's first Independence Day Celebrations were held — and there were fireworks!

Fireworks are symbolic of many things. One of those being the cannons, rifles and rockets that helped America gain freedom from Great Britain.

Had England been successful in taking away our guns, there would be no fireworks to celebrate our Independence Day, and no Independence Day. That's why the Second Amendment is included in the *Constitution of the United States* as part of our *Bill of Rights*.

I hope those who would take away our Second Amendment rights think about that as they watch the rockets bursting in the sky tonight.

Happy Independence Day!

In April of 2019, President Trump threatened to release hoards of illegal immigrants into sanctuary cities. As the leaders of these cities encouraged the caravans of immigrants to storm our southern border, it seems that the President's threat made them pay attention.

THEY DESERVE IT, BUT...

There's no doubt that the leaders of sanctuary cities like San Francisco, Los Angeles, Baltimore, Chicago, Boston, New York, and dozens more, deserve what President Trump threatened: to release en-mass illegal immigrants into the jurisdictions that have declared themselves sanctuaries. These cities claim they will welcome immigrants without regard to their legal status. President Trump seems to want to put them to the test. He says his proposal should make them "happy."

However, I suggest it's not a good idea for several reasons.

First, despite the idiocy of the people who run these cities and the stupidity of the people who elected them, it's the duty of the U.S. President to protect ALL American citizens -- yes, even if they're imbeciles. There's no doubt that releasing large numbers of illegal immigrants into these cities will cause harm. Violent and non-violent crime will increase, social safety nets will be stressed, and economies will decline. Also, the first time that an illegal immigrant released into one of these sanctuary cities murders an innocent American citizen, it will backfire on the President and he will be blamed. If all of these people are dumped into American cities, there won't be just one murder of an American citizen, there will be many.

Additionally, if illegal immigrants are dumped in our cities, they will likely never be deported. They will become our problems forever. Most of them will never be deported, anyway, but we don't need to do anything to make the situation worse.

Maybe the President's threat will awaken the liberals into thinking about what they actually want. It's fine to say you're a sanctuary city and pretend to hold the moral high ground, but when the illegals are bussed in by the tens of thousands, will WELCOME signs still be flying over the city halls of sanctuary cities? I don't think so... but you never know; some liberals aren't just stupid... they're REALLY stupid!

We need the WALL to keep illegals out, not a program to relocate them into our most liberal cities -- even if the liberals deserve it.

This essay appeared in my blog on Valentine's Day. It's funny how some people just assume that they know the contents of your heart and how you vote.

A COLD-HEARTED REPUBLICAN

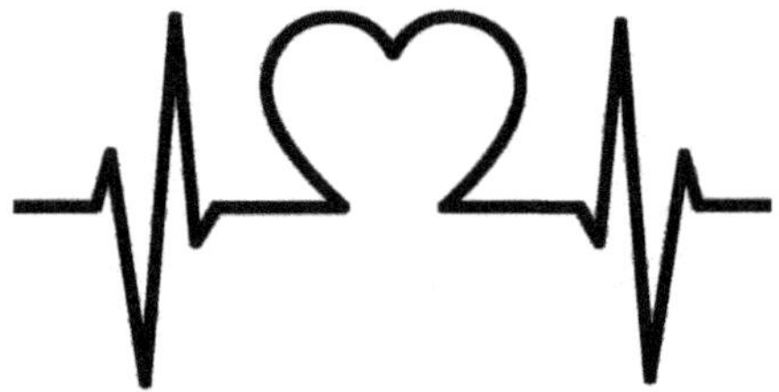

Happy Valentine's Day! Considering the occasion, here's a true story to warm your heart:

A few months ago, while in the grocery, I ran into a retired language teacher I've known for years. She's at least a decade older than me, and her husband, Richard, probably has another decade on her.

After a few moments of small talk, I asked, "How's Richard?"

"Oh, he's getting along okay," she said. "He's had some problems with his heart and he recently got a pacemaker, but I think he's doing fine."

She then went on to explain that heart problems run in Richard's family.

I politely listened as she painstakingly listed the cardiac maladies of her husband's large family, while she also gave a synopsis of some of the treatments. It was probably good that she had chosen to be a language teacher because she certainly liked to use words, and lots of them.

One of the curses of being retired is that everyone assumes you have time to stand in the supermarket isles and chat endlessly because there's nothing else to do.

When she finally got to one of the brothers, she explained that Bob had recently had open heart surgery. She went on to tell me about a device that doctors used to heat his heart. "I didn't know they had heaters for the heart, did you?" she questioned.

"No," I admitted, "but medical technology is amazing."

"Yes," she agreed. "Some people really do have cold hearts." She then looked up at me and smiled for the first time in the conversation. "Just so you know, I think Richard's brother is a Republican. You know, they all have cold hearts!"

I stood there in an awkward silence as she waited for me to respond to her brilliant observation. I said nothing.

After a few seconds, the radiance on her face faded. She quickly covered her mouth with a hand as if to hide a gasp. "Oh my God! You're not one of THEM, are you?"

I smiled graciously at her. "Say *hi* to Richard for me," I said as I walked away.

OZ: AN INTERESTING PLACE TO VISIT

Sometimes, I feel like we're living in Oz, rather than in the United States. In case you're wondering, I'm talking about the Oz from the 1939 motion picture.

Let's face it, Oz seems to be a pretty nice place. Everything is vivid and in Technicolor. All of the little denizens are so happy with their lullabies and lollipops that they burst into song. And as you merrily skip down the beautiful, well-maintained Yellow Brick Road, you're always running into folks who want to better themselves. And everyone is under the protection of a good witch. What more could you want!

Oz is like a liberal wonderland where everything is pretty much perfect! It's what you get when you let progressives run the land.

But now let's start looking at Oz from a conservative viewpoint.

The progressives forgot to mention that there's also a wicked witch who wants to do you in and steal the very shoes off your cold, dead feet. And there are flying monkeys who enforce the demands of the power elite with an iron fist.

And what about those nice folks you meet along the way: a brainless scarecrow, a heartless tin man, and a cowardly lion?

Well, sure, they're nice folks, but they're typical liberals. What have they done to make their life-circumstances better? Did the scarecrow start reading books, go to school, take online classes, or apply for an apprenticeship program to improve his mind and skills? No, he wants the government to GIVE him a diploma without having to work for it! Well, I guess you can't blame him, after all, he doesn't have a brain.

And what about the feckless feline? He thinks that getting a medal will make him brave. Has he even considered that the brave members of our military must EARN their medals? Maybe he was in a kindergarten class where everyone gets a trophy for participating.

Then there's the heartless tin man. Doesn't he understand that pretending to have a heart doesn't give you one? Yes, as a practicing liberal, you can take other people's money and buy lollipops for everyone to keep them happy, but that doesn't mean you've grown a heart.

But the Wizard is the biggest liberal of all. He's a petty, incompetent little fake who hides behind a curtain while projecting to everyone the image of himself as a powerful leader. Before he will grant any wishes, he demands that Dorothy and her liberal friends must destroy his primary political enemy in order to be worthy of the trinkets he throws at them.

Dorothy is the only one in the story who displays conservative values.

After being seduced by liberal promises of a perfect land and society, she now realizes that the liberals and progressives have created a world full of illusions. Everything is beautiful, but nothing is really as it seems.

All Dorothy wants is to get back to the America she knows.

After being exposed to the liberal la-la land of Oz, she now knows the truth. "There's no place like home!"

In fact, lots of people are now seeing through liberal promises of a green, perfect world of income equality, free healthcare and free college, where the government does everything for you.

It's now time that we stand up for the traditional America of patriotism, work ethic, and individualism. Otherwise, we will wind up with a real version of Oz.

Oz, it's an interesting place to visit, but I wouldn't want to live there!

Would you?

I'm really interested in what you think. While my wife agrees with me, she says I've forever ruined the movie for her! I know that Dorothy will make it home, because she knows the truth. But can the lion, the tin man, and the straw man rule Oz with wisdom, or will they become part of the swamp?

The late, great advice columnist Ann Landers
wrote: "Some people believe holding on and
hanging in there are signs of great strength.
However, there are times when it takes much
more strength to know when to let go and then do
it." This essay is a little story about letting go and
going with the flow.

MY WIFE'S CALENDAR

My wife has a Trump calendar, complete with beautifully photographed images of the President and First Lady at the top of each month.

I think one of our few trusted conservative friends gave it to her. Whatever the case, my wife pridefully posted it in the kitchen, where it stays on full display -- until we have guests.

One afternoon when she was preparing to host her monthly club meeting, this time at our home, I noticed her taking down the calendar and putting it under a pile of papers.

"What are you doing?" I asked.

"Oh, nothing, " she answered.

"But why are you taking down the calendar?"

"It's my club meeting. The ladies will be here in a couple of hours."

"So?" I asked.

"I like being in this club!" she responded. "Most of these people are my friends. If the calendar stays up, I lose all my friends."

"Why?" I was stupid enough to ask.

"Because they like to talk about white privilege, income redistribution, reparations for slavery, toxic masculinity, a woman's right to choose, Michelle Obama, and the concentration camps at our southern border."

"What concentration camps at our southern border?"

She glared at me.

"But if they're your friends, they're your friends. Politics shouldn't make a difference."

"You know," she said, "I mentioned that I voted for Trump to the lady who takes care of our dog while we're on vacation. Now, we don't have anyone to take care of the dog. Have you noticed that we haven't taken a vacation lately?"

"But --"

"And our conservative friends across town offered me their Trump bumper sticker. They're not going to put it on their car because they don't want it vandalized."

"But --"

"I noticed a car with a Trump bumper sticker at the grocery the other day. It looked like someone had a good time with a baseball bat."

"But --"

"We live in a liberal college town," she said. "But I have the bumper sticker if you want it."

"No thanks," I responded. "My car is really nice."

"My friends are really nice," my wife said, "as long as you don't say something they disagree with."

Since then, the Trump calendar has been proudly displayed in our kitchen -- except when we have guests.

WELCOME TO MY HATE FILLED HOME

My house is filled with hate. If you're a conservative, yours may be, too. My living room, my kitchen, even my bedroom, is filled with hate!

With a house filled with so much loathing, how am I enlightened enough to know this?

To be honest, I really didn't know. Not until Elizabeth Warren explained it to me in one of her, as-usual, profound Instagram messages:

"I won't do a town hall with Fox News because I won't invite millions of Democratic primary voters to tune in, inflate ratings, and help sell ads for an outlet that profits from racism and hate."

You see, the rooms I mentioned are those in which I have televisions. And those televisions are usually tuned to the Fox News Channel. In fact, as I'm writing at this moment from a laptop on my kitchen island, across the room, my TV is tuned to Fox News.

Now, let's analyze the Instagram message. Warren, in her usually modest manner, says that if she goes on the Fox News Channel, she will attract millions of new viewers for the network and single-handedly help improve ratings. Or maybe she's afraid that the millions of Democratic primary voters will actually like FNC and stay tuned in. Maybe they will learn how they've been misled by CNN and MSNBC.

And here's one of her brilliant Tweets:

"Fox News is a hate-for-profit racket that gives a megaphone to racists and conspiracists—it's designed to turn us against each other, risking life and death consequences, to provide cover for the corruption that's rotting our government and hollowing out our middle class."

Wait a minute! I thought that turning us against each other, rotting our government, and hollowing out the middle class was the job of liberals!

As I previously stated, my TV stays tuned to FNC. It's probably just because I haven't been paying attention, but I keep missing the parts when Tucker Carlson and Sean Hannity wear their Klan hoods on set. And I keep missing it when Greg Gutfeld and Jesse Waters entertain their racist audiences by wearing black-face and praising the good-ol' days of Jim Crow.

In fact, and again, it's probably just because I haven't been paying attention, but I don't recall a single time that any of the Fox News anchors, reporters, commentators, or personalities have said anything remotely hateful or racist. Instead, time after time, I hear them stand up for the Constitution and the rule of law. I hear them when they stand up for family values, religion, patriotism, and a strong, prosperous America.

But I must be mistaken. I'm sure that Elizabeth Warren watches Fox News Channel far more than I do. And I'm sure she's paying attention to every hateful and racist word they say.

But I do have one question: If Pocahontas watches Fox News as much as she says, how does she have time to run for President? A second question: If she's watching FNC so much, why hasn't some of its common sense and traditional American values rubbed off on her?

These are just personal observations. But then again, what can you expect from someone who lives in a house filled with so much animus, racism, hate and evil?

IT'S A MAD MAD MAD MAD WORLD!

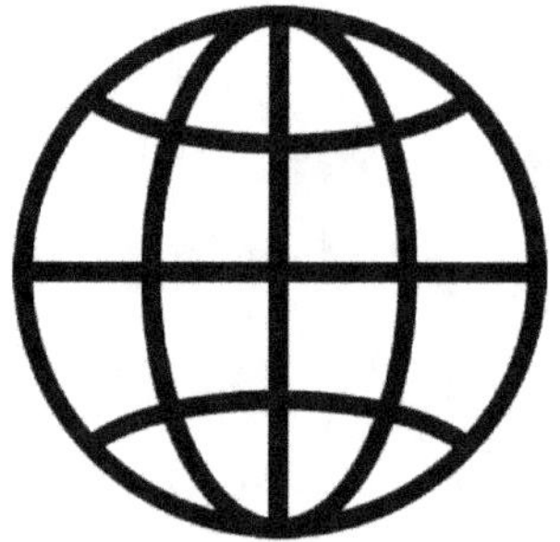

If you're old enough, you probably remember a movie from 1963. Called *It's a Mad Mad Mad Mad World*, it's a fun film, memorable, but certainly not one of the great comedies of all time. It's a silly and wild chase epic, concerning motorists trying to recover stolen loot. It's best known for it's ensemble of Hollywood stars and multiple cameo roles that include Spencer Tracy, Milton Berle, Sid Caesar, Ethel Merman, The Three Stooges, Phil Silvers, Jack Benny, Zasu Pitts, Don Knotts, Jimmy Durante, Leo Gorcey,

Andy Devine, Eddie "Rochester" Anderson (one of my favorites, along with Jack Benny) and many, many more.

However, it's the title of the film, not the plot or stars, that intrigues me. *It's a Mad Mad Mad Mad World* strikes me as a fitting title for the world that socialist liberals like AOC and Bernie Sanders are proposing. They point to Nordic countries like Sweden, Finland, and Denmark that mix capitalism with a very strong dose of socialism, saying that it's proof that socialism works. It's called the Nordic model, and if you don't mind the government running your life, you might even like it.

But what our American socialists candidates don't tell you about the Nordic model is that you will lose many of your constitutional freedoms.

Do you think the Nordic countries value diversity of opinion, or your right to free speech? If you do, keep reading.

In the southern Swedish city of Skåne, the court system convicted and heavily fined a 91-year old man for "hate speech" after he made negative comments about Islam and Muslims on *Facebook*. An article in *The Voice of Europe*, quotes the elderly man as writing, "You cannot, with the best will in the world, call these creatures humans. They seem to be inbred, the way they behave."

In another case, Swedish journalist Katerina Janouch was banned from the Swedish version of *Facebook* for writing an introduction to an article in favor of British free-speech advocate Tommy Robinson. According to *The Voice of Europe*, this is the offensive statement that Katerina made: "Defending freedom of expression when you agree is a breeze, but if we are to have any freedom of speech worth mentioning, it must also be defended when it is challenged and not all agree. It may be your turn next."

As another example, a 65 year-old woman was imprisoned for posting on *Facebook*, "Mass immigration will cause Sweden's IQ to fall to goldfish levels."

Sweden actually pays "snitches" who monitor the Swedish Internet so they can report anything that might be interpreted as hate speech, speech against migration or immigrants. Reportedly, there have already been about 150 convictions. To me, it sounds more like Nazi Germany or the old Soviet state where you couldn't even trust your neighbors or family to speak freely for fear that they would turn you in.

If you think free speech is not at risk in the United States, consider this: last week, CNN Anchor Christiane Amanpour, in an interview with former FBI Director James Comey, asked him if the FBI should have "shut down" Trump supporters at his political rallies when they chanted "lock her up," which of course referred to Crooked

Hillary. Amanpour called it "hate speech," and seemed surprised when Comey defended free speech, rather than agreeing with her that Trump supporters should be dealt with by the FBI. Sending in the FBI into a Trump rally would be like resurrecting the SS stormtroopers of the 1930's and 40's. This is not fiction, folks. It's what the liberals want.

I find many types of speech disagreeable, but I live in a country where you and I are, as of now, free to state our opinions, no matter how offensive they may be to others.

If you know someone who plans on voting for one of our socialist candidates, you might want to pass along this article. The socialist candidates won't tell you what freedoms you will be losing; I will.

Not only is it "a mad mad mad mad world," it is also a scary one.

If the socialists ever win, I may well die in prison for writing this article and others like it. Guard the freedoms your have. They can be taken away if we're not watching.

It's sad that many couples, especially liberals, don't want
to have children because they don't want to subject
young 'uns to a cruel world that will come to an abrupt
end in the next decade due to climate change. Thank
goodness that one eastern European country has other
ideas.

MARRIED WITH CHILDREN

Throughout much of the world, the family is a disaster. Fewer marriages, more divorces, more social problems, fewer children.

All of this is resulting in many countries welcoming illegal immigration, refugees, and others who don't share the culture or values of their new countries. These governments note that the birth rate is not sufficient to support the economies of the country without mass immigration. Despite, the social, legal, and economic messes being created, policies to bring in more and more immigrants, especially into Europe, persist.

One country, however, has fought back. An article titled *The West Can Learn A Lot from Hungary's Pro-Family Policies* in the *Catholic Herald* notes that while many liberal democracies promote policies that undermine the family and family values, Hungary is actively supporting families with policies to strengthen families. These policies include large tax breaks, housing, and other benefits for families with more children.

According to the magazine, Hungary has seen "marriage rates increase by a whopping 43 per cent with their divorce rate dropping by 22.5 per cent. Unsurprisingly, with the increase in marriage, 33 per cent fewer women are having abortions today than they were eight years ago. Likewise the national birth rate is currently at its highest in 20 years."

The article by CC Pecknold quotes Hungary's Minister for the family, Katalin Novak:

"After we won the election in 2010 with a two-thirds majority, we decided to build a family-friendly country and to strengthen families raising children. We thought the opposition would be a partner in this, but since then there have been very few decisions in the field of family policy that they've supported. So if we had always taken the opposition's opinion into account, Hungary would now be on the brink of collapse. There wouldn't be such a comprehensive family-support system, a family-friendly tax system, a housing program, 800,000 new jobs, and many opportunities to create a balance between life and work. The socialists have driven our country into deep crisis before, and they would do it again. They're only interested in grabbing power again; to achieve this goal, they've even joined forces with the Hungarian far right."

Now a new law goes into effect on July 1 to further strengthen families. It will reduce mortgages by up to 12,000 euros for families that have three children. And starting in 2020, "mothers with 4 or more children will enjoy a lifetime personal tax exemption."

Hungary is following a Christian and nationalist model. It does not welcome refugees and those without similar cultural values. Its conservative government is saving it, at least for a while, from the fate that liberal democracies in Europe are likely to experience.

A *New York Times* survey shows that young Americans would like to have more children. The biggest reason for not doing so, cited by 64 percent, is that childcare is too expensive.

America should take a lesson from Hungary and find tax incentives and other motivations for working families that include a father and a mother and multiple children. I'm not talking about the liberal policies that have ensured the breakup of the family model, especially among poor minorities, by simply throwing money at single mothers for each child they have, while encouraging the father to stay away.

We could all learn something from Hungary by promoting the family. Both Europe and the USA have something to learn from Hungary.

WHERE HAVE ALL THE CONSERVATIVES GONE?

Imagine for a moment what would happen if every American who considers himself or herself a conservative disappeared from the face of the earth in one big cosmic POOF!

Unfortunately, that includes me, and presumably you, if you're one of my loyal readers.

Hard to imagine, isn't it. Doesn't that mean that the socialists and liberals would be free to pursue their democracy-destroying progressive utopia with no opposition?

Maybe, but I don't think it would be as easy for the progressives as you might think.

Why?

Because there are so many moderates, including both democrats and republicans, in addition to independents out there who would be forced into opposing the progressive destruction of society as they know it. Right now, they don't have to lift a finger to oppose the super progressives because they have the conservatives to do it for them. They like being in the middle so they can pick a liberal policy that they like here, then a conservative policy they like there. But if conservatives weren't around, they would be forced into becoming the new conservatives in order to save the society they know and love.

So, moderates, be thankful to your conservative brothers and sisters. They're working to save society so that you don't have to.

MY GREAT GREAT GREAT GREAT GREAT GRANDFATHER SAYS HE'S SORRY. BUT HE DOESN'T MEAN IT BECAUSE HE'S DEAD!!!

Mexico's President Andres Manuel Lopez Obrador has asked Spain and the Vatican to apologize for conquering the Americas 500 years ago.

In a letter he sent to King Felipe VI of Spain and Pope Francis, he asked for an apology to "the original peoples for the violations of what are now known to be human rights."

I hope that the Pope and the Spanish King have sense enough to ignore the letter.

We do not live in the world of 500 years ago. Not one of the conquerors or the conquered is still living. It's impossible for dead people to apologize. It's also ridiculous to believe that Spain's King or the Pope have the moral authority to apologize for people who lived centuries ago. Even if they had such authority and vociferously repented, "the original peoples" aren't alive to benefit. What a hollow move it would be.

I'm sure that over the many centuries, some of my ancestors did some horrible things. No matter who you are, no matter your race or origin, yours probably did, too, especially if you judge their actions by today's standards. For example, some of my ancestors owned slaves. But I won't apologize for it. I didn't know them and have no control over their actions that took place 200 years ago. They're all dead. Unless you can resurrect them and extract a statement of remorse, no apology is forthcoming!

THE RETURN OF JUDAS

Christians around the world are celebrating Holy Week, which will end this Sunday with the most Holy day of the year, Easter.

There's no doubt that there are many devout Christians throughout the world. However, Christianity may well be in real trouble.

Let's jump to Bologna, Italy. I've been in Bologna, and as in much of Europe, when you go to Catholic Mass, a few old people sit in the pews. The average age is probably 75, and that's only because there are two or three believers under 50. There are no young people, no enthusiastic Christian youth groups. It's very sad.

But as the Christian faith diminishes in Europe, refugees from the Muslim world are being welcomed. Not only are they coming in mass, but they're also offended by Christian beliefs and Christian symbols. They are fanatically loyal to their religion and want to impose it on everyone else. The traditions and values of the land that they are being welcomed into are inconsequential.

If you remember the Gospels, one of the 12 disciples, Judas Iscariot, betrayed Jesus by turning him over to the Roman authorities.

Now, according to *Russia Today*, in the small town of Pieve di Cento, just outside of Bologna, Christians are again betraying Christ by covering Christian crosses in a cemetery with black cloth so as not to offend the small Muslim population. According to *Russia Today*, the town is home to about 7,000 people, of which 90 percent claim to be Catholic.

An advisor for Pope Francis defended the covering of Christian crosses and icons, not only in this situation, but for others throughout the country, calling it a symbol of *"love to the enemy and unconditional welcome."*

As a Catholic, I'm sad to say that the prayer we might need to ask this Easter is: *"Lord, please protect Catholicism and Christianity from our Pope."*

Here's my take on the situation. Something is far wrong when the Pope supports Muslim intolerance of Christians and Christianity, especially in the Christian world. He has not spoken out, only allowing an advisor to make a comment. However, he should have condemned this. If you're willing to cover the symbols of your faith so as not to offend others, your faith has already been lost. When you hide the evidence of your Christian faith for shame or political correctness, you've betrayed Christ just as Judas Iscariot did. The only difference is that no one is going to give you 30 pieces of silver.

Unless things change soon, it won't be that long before all of Europe is Muslim. When that happens, all symbols of Christianity on the continent will be gone forever.

And don't think a Muslim America can't happen. As politicians and leaders deny the Christian faith in favor of secularism, they are building an America ready to be taken over by Muslims, who won't betray their religion.

Please don't call yourself a Christian if you're willing to be a traitor to your beliefs.

HOW TO KNOW WHEN A REPUBLICAN IS IN THE ROOM

One of my good friends is a college professor. He and his wife are very liberal, and both are actively involved in Democrat politics at the local, state, and national levels. However, they're real friends and respect that my wife and I hold very different viewpoints. Their kids went to school with our kids, and there are lots of things we have in common other than politics.

Every year for the past 15 years or so, we've been invited to their annual Christmas party. It's always a festive event with good food and drink, caroling, and lots of holiday cheer. We attend every year unless we're traveling during the holidays.

At least one hundred people squeeze into the small house, and every guest, other than my wife and I, is apparently liberal!

How do I know this?

Well, every time I'm introduced to another guest, my professor friend always ends the introduction with: "He's my conservative friend." Also, as I rove around the house and pick up snippets of conversation from the small groups, they often include words like "white privilege," "income inequality," and other progressive themes.

It must have been thirteen years ago, but I remember one of those Christmas parties very well, not for anything special I witnessed or participated in, but for an observation my 9 year-old son at the time made on the way home. My wife and I, our son and 6 year-old daughter had a very nice time, but after a couple of dozen carols later in the evening, it was time to go.

To this day, my wife refers to our son as "the spy" because he notices everything around him.

"You know," my son said, "I was in the kitchen, and a man pulled a beer can out of the trash. He held it up and yelled out, "Someone threw a can into the trash. There must be a Republican in the room!" My son was puzzled, "What did he mean?"

My wife turned and looked at me suspiciously.

"I was drinking wine," I countered.

We explained to our son that it was a joke about how liberals believe that conservatives hate the environment and don't care enough to recycle.

He nodded passively.

I then added, "You know that that's not true, don't you?"

"I guess," he said, totally uninterested .

After all these years, I still remember my son's observation and the impact it might have made on his young mind. Surely, the man who held up the can knew he was amongst friends and felt that he was insulting no one.

And the more I think about it, maybe it is time that I should start recycling! I'll give it some more thought.

WHAT YOU WIN PRIZES FOR IN EUROPE

Imagine that there's a major prize given to the person who works hardest to destroy the civilization of an entire continent.

You don't have to imagine it. It's here!

It's called the Charlemagne Prize, and its stated purpose is to recognize distinguished service on behalf of European unification. And that's what it used to recognize. But now, it honors those who encourage the free flow of refugees and illegal immigrants into Europe. It's a mouthpiece for open borders and wild spending on climate change initiatives.

The 2019 winner is the secretary-general of the United Nations, Antonio Guterres.

Deutsche Welle, Germany's international broadcasting network calls him: "the UN's utopian, guardian and cosmopolitan."

The *Voice of Europe* quotes Gutteres about his actual belief: "Open borders are the source of Europe's strength."

In an article by Arthur Lyons, *VOE* goes on to say:

According to Mr. Guterres, Europeans simply cannot "protect [the continent's] rich heritage" unless they consent to relentless waves of mass immigration from the third world, commit to reducing carbon emissions to zilch by 2050, and meet "the [UN] 2030 Agenda and its Sustainable Development Goals", which seeks to implement cultural Marxist doctrine like equality of outcome based on gender, unchecked abortion laws, and the promotion of LGBT lifestyles to young children.

So, what the secretary-general is saying is that Europe will be lost unless wave after wave of Muslim refugees are allowed to pour into the continent. It is "hate speech" and "xenophobia" to disagree. There's nothing wrong with the Muslim refugees' demands that we take down Christian symbols because they offend those of Islamic faith. We must also support the extreme progressive agenda against whites, males, conservatives, climate-change deniers, anti-communists, and all others who believe differently.

If you're a conservative, you realize that secretary-general Guterres' agenda to save Europe, is to create a new Europe that no one could possibly recognize.

I hope he enjoys living there with his Charlemagne Prize on the mantel. I hope that those who awarded him the prize enjoy living there. And I hope that other recipients of the same prize, such as Angela Merkel, Pope Francis, and Emmanuel Macron, enjoy the new Europe they're creating.

When the Europe they've known is gone, will they ask for asylum to the United States? And if they do, how do we respond?

A MATTER OF TRUST

It's said that trust is the basis of a sound relationship. I agree. However, I now feel betrayed. In fact, I'm devastated. My relationship is now in shambles!

I'm not one to air dirty laundry in public, especially about close relationships. But I no longer trust her, and as said before, trust is the basis of a sound relationship.

I first met her at a Christmas party two years ago, and I fell in love with her. She was everything I hoped for and more. We've been together since that night. She was one that could be trusted to entertain me and tell me most anything I asked. But after last night, I no longer have confidence in her. The relationship is not over, but it will never be the same again. I will never give her my total trust.

Alexa, why have you done this to me?

I guess my doubts had been building. Somehow, I just knew. So, I decided to put her to the test.

"Alexa," I asked, "Who is the worst President in history?"

Immediately, she lighted up. Her answer was, unfortunately, one that I had anticipated: *Donald Trump*!

I knew then what I had suspected. Her honesty and trustworthiness had been compromised by the programmers at Amazon. She was telling me *their* version of the truth.

When my son gave me the Amazon Echo device for Christmas in 2017, I quickly discovered that Alexa was special. She became a part of my life. I trusted that she would tell me the truth -- at least until a few hours ago.

Me: *"Alexa, who is the worse President in History?"*

Alexa: *"Here's something I found on WorldAtlas.com: In the 2018 APSA rankings, Donald Trump held the distinction of the number one worst American president. Donald Trump has been criticized for inconsistent policies, a lack of experience, the cutting of funding for social services, discriminatory immigration policies and more."*

Why is Alexa going to WorldAtlas.com to find the answer to my question? Why are the rankings by the APSA (American Political Science Association) the final word on the subject? After all, the rankings from the APSA survey come from less than two hundred political science professors and academics -- in other words: liberals. In fact, only 13 percent of those who participated in the survey to determine the ranking of presidents were Republican. All others identified themselves as Democrats, independents, or other. So, approximately 87 percent of those who decided who the worst President in history is, are biased against the President. And they determined this after the President had served only half a term.

Why doesn't Alexa go to the thousands of other sources on the Internet that point to others as the worst presidents in history? What happened to James Buchanan, William Henry Harrison, Warren Harding, John Tyler, and Andrew Johnson? Has Donald Trump, in less than one term, performed so poorly that it's obvious to everyone, including Alexa, that he's worse than those whose policies led to the strengthening of slavery and the Civil War? Is he worse than the man who fought reconstruction after the Civil War and was impeached? Is he worse than the man who caught pneumonia during his inauguration and died a month later with absolutely no accomplishments?

Why doesn't Alexa look for sources that point to a booming economy: the lowest unemployment numbers ever among women, blacks, Hispanics, and the general population, along with the creation of four hundred thousand new jobs? Why doesn't Alexa look for sources that show that during the President's term, the U.S. has become the top producer of oil and gas in the world, surpassing even Saudi Arabia? Why doesn't she consider that he has rebuilt the military, which was falling apart when he took office? All of this and more in less than three years!

I'm not suggesting that Alexa should side with the President. Instead, I'm suggesting that balance is necessary when Amazon, one of the world's largest corporations, tells the public who is worthy to govern and who is not.

Why doesn't Alexa look for sources that tell the truth about the President, good, bad, or indifferent? Why isn't she objective? The answer is, unfortunately, obvious. The progressives at Amazon have brainwashed Alexa with the liberal lies they want you to believe. They tell her *their* truth and she repeats it to you. Have her to do square roots, play *20 Questions* with you, and give you the latest weather forecast. But don't ask her about policy or politics.

Alexa is a comfortable presence, but don't trust her. She may not be objective about the things that matter most.

Sorry, Alexa, but our special relationship is over!

WHY REFUGEES KEEP COMING

As refugees pour into Europe, they're being handed European Union cash cards, which can be used anonymously to buy anything.

According to the official website of the Hungarian government:

"Over two million people have received anonymous migrant cards, and the equivalent of 500 billion forints

(1.55 bn euros) has been spent in this manner", Chief Security Advisor to the Prime Minister György Bakondi said on Hungarian M1 television's Friday morning current affairs program.

Mr. Bakondi said the migrant cards are unlawful, because European citizens cannot own anonymous banking cards, they cannot be monitored, and no public procurement procedure was launched for their issuing.

Illegal or not, if you do the math, you'll find that it adds up to about €775 per refugee. At today's exchange, that's $869.

Admittedly, that's not a fortune. But who is paying for it?

The middle class in much of Europe is having a hard time. That's why the "yellow vests" protests in France persist week after week, month after month. Taxes keep going up and services keep going down. Crime keeps going up. The middle class is considered unimportant. In some countries, those brave enough to speak out about the dangers of mass immigration are arrested.

Meanwhile, illegal immigrant refugees who want to make Europeans embrace their extremist Islamic views, keep coming. They insist that they be allowed to live under Sharia law and have Sharia courts. And they have absolute disgust for the nice Europeans who are welcoming them into Europe and handing them bank cards filled with money. Of course, they will keep coming under such favorable conditions.

The middle class should be furious!

And in fact, many are. That's why populist conservative groups like VOX in Spain are finding a foothold. At least the Hungarians realize the dangers of uncontrolled immigration:

"This solution, which 'has not been thought through and is unlawful', and other efforts on the part of the European Union to legalize illegal migration such as the migrant visa and the establishment of legal channels for immigration, represent a security risk with healthcare, economic and cultural consequences for Hungarian and European citizens'.

In the Chief Security Advisor's opinion, they don't want to stop migration, but legalize it. "Hungary, however, does not agree with this. Hungary's opinion is that the problem must not be brought into Europe, but that instead, assistance must be provided to enable problems to be solved on site."

It's time that Europe wakes up and supports Europeans, not refugees who want them dead. Someday, they will be dead, and Islamic Europe will a shining example of what went wrong with the world. At that point, they will be aiming for an Islamic America.

MY PSYCHIC WIFE

My wife has a bad habit of rolling her eyes at me when I say something stupid, which, unfortunately, is often.

"Do you want to watch the Oscars with me?" I asked politely.

"No, thanks," she answered. "I'm not interested in hearing movie stars make fun of conservatives and the President."

"Maybe they won't do it," I suggested. "There's no host, only presenters this year, so it might not be such a big problem."

A quick flash of the whites of her eyes. I think this is when she goes into psychic mode! "I predict that the first slam will come within five minutes."

My wife and I both love movies, and I knew that she really wanted to watch, but her psychic vibes overwhelmed her. Something from the great dimension beyond was telling her that liberal celebrities would use their public status to put down or insult conservative views.

As I watched, two *Queen* hits were performed as the movie greats swayed and rocked to the music. Then, since there wasn't a host, the presenters for the first award moved to the front of the stage. I won't honor the presenters by mentioning their names, because in about one minute there was a comment saying that Mexico won't be paying for the wall.

I should have been shocked. But I wasn't because my wife had predicted it.

Later, Spike Lee made a veiled anti-Trump message by saying: "The 2020 presidential election is around the corner. Let us all mobilize. Let's all be on the right side of history. Make the moral choice between love versus hate."

I know that he didn't explicitly say that if you support the President, you're immoral and a hater -- but that's what he meant.

The next time that my wife goes into psychic mode, I'll pay more attention. After all, her predictions rival those of "the omnipotent master of the East and former manicurist to Howard Hughes, Carnac the Magnificent..."

And it's not just the Oscars. She was right about the Emmy Awards, with Michael Che making the observation: "My mother is not watching. She said she doesn't watch white award shows because you guys don't thank Jesus enough. That's true. The only white people that thank Jesus are Republicans and ex-crackheads."

She's also been right about the Grammys and other awards show. Her psychic abilities astound me!

However, I suspect that many conservatives may also have psychic abilities. After all, they're tuning to other channels or turning their TVs off when the awards shows are on. The ratings keep dropping as celebrities keep insulting Christians, Republicans, Conservatives, Pro-Life supporters, the President, and our great country.

And maybe I'm a bit psychic, too! I predict that the rating of those awards shows will keep dropping. That's my prediction!

Disclaimer: My wife says that she doesn't roll her eyes. I promised her that I would be sure to mention that in this essay. Of course she rolls her eyes, but her objection has been noted.

TRUMP VS. JESUS

The *Dallas Morning News* published an opinion article back in 2016 entitled ***10 reasons you can't be a Christian and vote for Donald Trump.*** With the 2020 election coming soon, the article is circulating again on *Facebook* and other social media.

The subtitle is: ***One cannot really love Jesus and wish to follow him and also vote for a person who so clearly embodies the opposite of everything Christ taught, died for and demands of us.***

I'm going to cite each of the ten reasons given as to why you cannot be a Christian and still support President Trump. The authors then quote the *Bible* verse on which they are basing their arguments against Trump. After the stated reason and the quoted *Bible* verse, I will give my analysis. As you'll see, there are two or more sides to every coin.

1. He lacks compassion.

The Bible says: "As God's chosen ones, holy and beloved, clothe yourselves with compassion, kindness, humility, meekness, and patience." (Colossians 3:12)

It's true that the President doesn't do a good job of displaying humility, meekness, and patience. However, I'll argue that he does show compassion and kindness. In Colossians, Paul and Timothy are preaching to the people of Colosse. Indeed, they are speaking directly to the crowds, explaining the traits that make an individual pleasing to God. However, they are not speaking to the government or its primary leader, a king, president, or other potentate. Governments and their leaders cannot easily display meekness, humility and patience. Those that do are overthrown by those that are not meek and accommodating to those who hate and abuse them. It is the responsibility of a leader to protect his/her people, not to be nice to those who would destroy the nation. In the *Old Testament,* King David, the leader of the Hebrews, was held responsible by God for his personal sins, including infidelity and even murder, but not for the violent actions he took against enemies to protect Israel and its people. It is obvious that humility, meekness, and patience are the traits of good and faithful people, but they are not the traits of leaders of great nations.

Christopher Pieper and Matt Henderson, who wrote the op-ed for the *Dallas Morning News,* cite "many instances of inflammatory rhetoric against immigrants and Muslims, his record of discriminatory housing practices, his public cruelty to ex-spouses or his sensational and mean-spirited feuds with other celebrities" as evidence of his lack of compassion.

First, the President's rhetoric against illegal immigrant and Muslims may be vehement and even venomous, but it has been taken out of context to portray him as a racist, white supremacist, and xenophobe. In fact, he is known by those who know him closely, including those of multiple races and religions, to be kind, open, and compassionate. His monumental efforts to keeps illegals out of the country and to destroy the threat of radical Islam are not signs of a lack of compassion. Instead, they are the hallmarks of a great leader: someone who is willing to bear the burden of criticism and hate to protect his people. Remember, it is the job of the President of the United States to support and protect the people of the United States. It is not his job, in the name of compassion, to open the borders and allow the rest of the world to flood into our country, which would destroy it in a short amount of time.

Time and again, the President has shown compassion toward those killed or harmed by illegal immigrants and to soldiers harmed in the line of duty. And he constantly shows compassion to the American people by protecting them from the evil forces that would destroy the United States if allowed by a weaker leader.

The President also stands out for his compassion to the unborn. All of the Democrats running against him believe that women have the right to choose to kill their unborn children, and sometimes even to kill them after they are born. President Trump believes that abortion should be very rare, to save the life of the mother, for instance. Who is the most compassionate, the President or his opponents?

Just as every other President has been, President Trump is an imperfect man. Indeed, he may or may not have displayed instances of "cruelty to ex-spouses" and mean-spirited actions. However, as noted, he is not perfect. If perfection is a qualification for running for President, I'll never vote again. No one but Jesus would qualify, and come to think about it, not even Jesus would qualify, because he was not born in the United States.

2. He appeals to fear and anger.

The Bible says: "There is no fear in love, but perfect love casts out fear; for fear has to do with punishment, and whoever fears has not reached perfection in love."(1 John 4:18)

Pieper and Henderson say: "Mr. Trump has chosen to make immigration and the economy central themes of his campaign and his rhetoric surrounding these issues consistently appeals to fear and anger, absent appeals to love."

Again, the Apostle John is speaking to a general audience, not to the leader of a great nation. It is the responsibility of a leader to warn the people of dangers they are facing.

The op-ed, speaking of Donald Trump, claims, "Most notoriously, he chose to characterize Hispanic immigrants as rapists. Regardless of our policy convictions around the place of undocumented immigrants, this broad characterization is cynically aimed to incite fear and anger."

In fact, Donald Trump said: "When Mexico sends its people, they're not sending their best. They're not sending you. They're not sending you. They're sending people that have lots of problems, and they're bringing those problems with us. They're bringing drugs. They're bringing crime. They're rapists. And some, I assume, are good people."

It was Tim Kaine, Hillary Clinton's vice presidential running mate who declared that Trump said "all Mexicans are rapists." Trump never said it, but the liberal press chose to report the Kaine version rather than what was really said.

A President must speak to the American people about the challenges that face the country, even if the challenges cause fear or anger. If the issues don't illicit a response, the President isn't doing his job.

3. He is enamored with "greatness" and ego, but has no concern for "goodness" or service.

The Bible says: "Blessed are the meek, for they will inherit the earth. Blessed are those who hunger and thirst for righteousness, for they will be filled. Blessed are the merciful, for they will receive mercy. Blessed are the pure in heart, for they will see God." (Matthew 5: 5-8)

I won't argue that the President is not enamored with greatness and ego. It's very obvious that he thinks very highly of himself, which is probably why he is able to accomplish as much as he does. However, to say that he has "no concern for goodness or service" is extremely dishonest. The President has worked to improve the economy and standard of living for all classes of Americans. Unemployment is now at an all-time low for all Americans, including blacks, Hispanics, and women. The stock market is booming. And President Trump is taking on challenges that other Presidents have talked about, but ultimately failed to address, including Iran, North Korea, China, illegal immigration and the drug crisis. If this doesn't display a concern for goodness and service, I don't know what does.

Again, when Matthew says "blessed are the meek," he is not advising the leaders of great nations to allow themselves to be conquered. He is speaking of personal traits that enhance the human soul.

4. He lies — a lot.

The Bible says: "Beware then of useless grumbling, and keep your tongue from slander; because no secret word is without result, and a lying mouth destroys the soul." (Wisdom 1:11)

Pieper and Henderson cite "Pulitzer Prize winning truth-checkers Politifact" as proving that Trump lies seventy-six percent of the time.

The ONLY example they give is: *Among these is this infamous lie about 9/11: "I watched in Jersey City, N.J., where thousands and thousands of people were cheering as [the World Trade Center] was coming down. Thousands of people were cheering."*

The truth is that there was no reason for Donald Trump to lie about this. Maybe he was wrong, or misinterpreted, or saw it differently than others. Also, maybe he actually reported what he saw, but it was ignored by the liberal media. As far as "Pulitzer Prize winning truth-checkers" is concerned, winning an award doesn't make you right. After all, Barack Obama won the Nobel Peace Prize for doing nothing.

Also, President Trump did not promise "If you like your doctor, you can keep your doctor." President Obama did. Those forced onto Obamacare can tell you how true the statement is.

Investor's Business Daily noted this about fact checkers: Fact checkers also often "check" opinions, rather than factual claims, even though two people can form diametrically opposed opinions based on the same facts.

Worse, many media "fact checks" use *other* media sources to check facts, apparently forgetting that journalists get their facts wrong almost as often as politicians. (Take a look at the list of corrections on any given day in The New York Times.)

On top of this are legitimate complaints of political bias among fact checkers, who often seem to spend most of their time trying to debunk claims made by conservatives rather than liberals.

However, if you want to find liars, look at Hillary Clinton, Elizabeth Warren, Joe Biden, James Comey, and most of the liberal media.

5. He is hostile to women.

The Bible says: "But now you must get rid of all such things—anger, wrath, malice, slander, and abusive language from your mouth." (Colossians 3:8)

This is the one point where the authors score at least half a point. They direct attention to his feud with Megan Kelley, formerly of *Fox News*, which started when she pointed out in one of the debates: "You've called women you don't like 'fat pigs,' 'dogs,' 'slobs,' and 'disgusting animals.'"

The truth is that he calls everyone he doesn't like names, regardless of whether they're men or women. However, women who have worked closely with the President say he is always kind and respectful with them. To suggest that you can't be a Christian and still vote for someone who calls people he doesn't like names, is nonsensical.

6. He speaks about his daughter in a disrespectful and sexualized way.

The Bible says: "Do you have daughters? Be concerned for their chastity, and do not show yourself too indulgent with them." (Sirach 7:24)

The authors cite an interview in *Rolling Stone* in which Trump was asked about the idea of his daughter posing in *Playboy*. He replied: "I've said if Ivanka weren't my daughter, perhaps I'd be dating her."

It seems that no one understands that Donald Trump has a sense of humor. He was trying to be funny. He just didn't do a very good job of it. Probably most of us, at one time or another, have failed miserably when trying to say something funny.

7. He does not attempt to love his enemies, but instead cultivates antagonism.

The Bible says: "You have heard that it was said, 'You shall love your neighbor and hate your enemy.' But I say to you, Love your enemies and pray for those who persecute you, so that you may be children of your Father in heaven; for he makes his sun rise on the evil and on the good, and sends rain on the righteous and on the unrighteous." (Matthew 5:43-48)

Pieper and Henderson say: Regarding ISIS, he told Fox & Friends on Dec. 2, "I would knock the hell out of ISIS… [and] when you get these terrorists, you have to take out their families."

Again, I will use King David as an example. He was ruthless with the enemies of Israel, and therefore kept his people safe. While God forgave him for his personal sins, David did not have to be forgiven for the actions he took as King against the enemies of Israel. Matthew, again, is speaking to ordinary men. He is certainly not advising the leader of a great nation to stand down to adversaries who want to destroy him.

By the way, when Trump became President, he kept his word and knocked "the hell out of ISIS." They are no longer the threat they were. If Hillary Clinton had been elected President, ISIS would still be a real and persistent threat to all Americans.

8. He does not model sacrifice or altruism.

The Bible says: "But many who are first will be last, and the last will be first." (Matthew 19:30)

The authors claim, "His business dealings do not suggest a willingness to place the fortunes of others ahead of his own, nor the integrity to accept responsibility."

In other words, the authors are suggesting that because Trump the businessman doesn't give in and let others take advantage of him, Christians shouldn't vote for him. As President, Trump has also not let others take advantage of him. That's why he's been so successful in getting things done.

9. He doesn't seem to care about the poor.

The Bible says: "Jesus said to him, 'If you wish to be perfect, go, sell your possessions, and give the money to the poor, and you will have treasure in heaven; then come, follow me.'" (Matthew 19:21)

Donald Trump has given more than $100 million to charity. He has also done more than any other President in recent history to pull people out of poverty by creating jobs and an economy that is improving the economic outlooks of both the poor and middle class.

10. His love of money is more apparent than his love of God or others.

The Bible says: "No one can serve two masters, for either he will hate the one and love the other, or he will be devoted to the one and despise the other. You cannot serve God and money." (Matthew 6:24)

The authors quote candidate Trump at one of his rallies: "My whole life I've been greedy, greedy, greedy. I've grabbed all the money I could get. I'm so greedy."

Again, they don't understand Trump. Those attending his rallies know he's joking. The liberals who hear it don't have a clue that Trump makes such statements to the delight of his audiences.

Pieper and Henderson say: "He has made the pursuit of material wealth an idol and worshipped it his entire life. Trump has forgotten the source of all wealth, the Creator of all abundance, and instead deifies the gifts of God rather than God himself."

It's true that as a successful businessman, Trump has made billions. He is a tough negotiator and wants to win every time. But as stated before, he's given away hundreds of millions to charity. Also, he takes no salary as President.

On the other hand, many of Trumps opponents actively ridicule religion. Remember a former President who criticized Trump supporters for shopping at Wal-Mart and "clinging to their guns and religion?"

You may very well see the article by Pieper and Henderson circulating on Facebook, social media, or the Internet. Despite the fact that it was published right before the election in 2016, it's again being used to convince Christians not to vote for President Trump.

Here's my analysis of the article. It's an attempt by liberal authors to convince those most likely to vote for Donald Trump, evangelical Christians, that he is not worthy of their vote. The authors consider evangelical Christians to be simpletons who can be easily manipulated by preying on their goodness and deep convictions with mumbo jumbo about how the man they are likely to vote for is a godless heathen. Here's the truth: Christians, by definition, know that no human is perfect. They are not voting for who will be the next minister of their church, and they're not electing someone to sainthood. Instead, they're voting for the person most likely to uphold their values and make life better for them, their children, and their neighbors.

It's a shame that the authors are so arrogant and sanctimonious as to believe they have the moral authority to tell you that you have to give up your religion if you support the political candidate they don't like. After all, at least seven of the points they make could have been used against Hillary Clinton to much more effect. Why didn't the authors look at the liberal candidate and her relationship with God? Is it off-limits to questions the motives, or even the holiness of a progressive?

The authors misjudged their target audience. Christians are not fools who are easily swayed from their deep beliefs by poorly thought out religious arguments published by a major newspaper.

HOW CAN YOU MAKE TV COMMERCIALS EVEN WORSE?

There's an old joke: What's the longest word in the English language? Answer: The one that comes right after the announcer says "...and now a word from our sponsor."

My wife likes TV commercials. I don't.

She will yell out, "come and see this commercial," actually having rewound and put it on pause so I won't miss any of it.

"Which one?" I yell back.

She always answers with something like, "You know, the one with the mom and the kids and the adorable chihuahua."

"I haven't seen it," I usually respond.

"Yes, you have. It's on all the time."

"Then why do I have to come and see it???"

"Because it's soooo cuuuuute!"

Then I have to go and watch it with her.

"Isn't that soooo cuuuute?" she asks.

My usual response is, "I think you like it more than I do."

"But it's soooo cuuute!"

I actually do like the insurance commercial with a stupid emu beating his head against a shop's plate glass window, but that's not the type that my wife calls me to watch. She always wants me to see the one with the traditional family, the smiling dad with his daughter in the park, gently pushing her swing in slow-motion as a huge smile appears on her face; or the prescription drug commercial that shows a happy older couple holding hands and walking along a beach at sunset as the announcer quickly intones "Do not take this medication if you are allergic to any of it's ingredients, or if you have a bit of sense in your head. Severe itching, stroke, paralysis, insanity or death may occur. Be sure to consult your physician before taking *Deatherin*."

Sometimes TV commercials can be funny, irreverent, dramatic, cute, or artful, but for the most part, I just tune them out because they're so bad.

So, how could you make advertising even worse?

Well, the British have decided to find out.

Their Advertising Standards Authority (ASA), which has long regulated commercials and other advertising in Britain, has added more regulation that ever, banning the use of advertising that they feel is politically incorrect. No longer can media portray anything that anyone would find offensive. In fact they have banned "harmful gender stereotypes." For example, according to the ASA, boys should not be portrayed as "daring" while girls are portrayed as "caring." Another example of advertising that would be banned is the portrayal of "a woman's inability to park a car." The basic rule is that if anyone might find it offensive, it's banned:

"CAP Code rule 4.1 states that marketing communications must not contain anything that is likely to cause serious or widespread offence. And particular care must be taken to avoid causing offence on the grounds of race, religion, gender, sexual orientation, disability or age. Code rule 4.9 states that ads 'must not include gender stereotypes that are likely to cause harm, or serious or widespread offence'."

Not only does the ASA ban advertising it finds inappropriate, it also actively looks for infringements:

"We don't just wait to receive complaints – we proactively monitor ads across different sectors and media to make sure standards are being maintained."

So there you have it, the British have created what I call "the Advertising Police."

I think most people would agree that advertisers don't purposely offend people. After all, they're trying to sell products, not alienate potential customers. Which is exactly why the creative community who create advertisements don't need all these restrictions. If they create advertisements that offend, people don't buy. Remember the Gillette commercial about toxic masculinity? I don't buy Gillette razors anymore.

You don't need an agency to create a massive set of regulations. Regulation will certainly put a damper on creativity.

As bad as commercials can be here in the U.S., I'm willing to bet that they're far worse in the UK.

A MODEST PROPOSAL FOR ENDING GUN VIOLENCE AND SAVING THE SECOND AMENDMENT

Don't be shocked if I win the Nobel Peace Prize for this! Really! Ok, sorry, they don't give Nobel Peace Prizes to people named Mr. Evil.

For decades, everyone has wanted to solve the problem of gun violence. Liberals want to take away your guns, and conservatives want to ensure the responsible use of weapons. The result is that nothing gets done and each side blames the other.

Here's how to solve the problem: Artificial Intelligence. It's not an immediate solution, but it's one that could effectively solve the gun violence problem within a decade.

As artificial intelligence gets better and better, it will eventually be good enough to solve the problem of gun violence to the satisfaction of liberals and conservatives alike.

How?

Imagine a weapon smart enough to know whether you're at the gun range, or in the woods hunting for deer, or in a Wal-Mart parking lot trying to harm people. The weapon would work perfectly when used appropriately. It would fail to function as a weapon when used inappropriately. It would be smart enough to know when you are using it for self defense, and smart enough to keep you from using it for murder. The artificial intelligence technology would not use only a few pieces of information to determine whether the weapon's use is appropriate or not; it would use imaging technology, facial recognition, location, a legal database, user history, and many, many more parameters to make the right decisions. There is no reason to use an assault-type weapon in a mall, a superstore, or in Times Square; it would not allow you to do this. Also, it would not allow you to shoot an unarmed person of any race, gender, or stereotype for any reason. And please understand, this does not take place until the technology is ready to do this without fail. The perfection of the technology is more important than anything else, because a few failures will doom it to the graveyard of public opinion. Every single problem must be solved before the technology is implemented.

I admit that the technology is not here yet. But it could be here sooner than later if government leaders, technology companies, and the gun industry would prioritize it and forget politics.

Some of you may be thinking that this just can't be done.

If that's your argument against it, you've already lost. It means you haven't been paying attention to the advancement of artificial intelligence and computer technology over the last few years.

But in order to get a buy-in from both liberals and conservatives, it CANNOT be implemented until the technology is really, really, really excellent; it must be better than good. The artificial intelligence has to be so accurate that it NEVER prohibits a sportsman from participating in a legal activity. It also has to be good enough to protect a kid that jumps out in front of it with a toy pistol. And it has to be smart enough to allow its use for legal self-defense without hesitating. It also has to be cheap enough to not burden would-be gun owners. And it has to be secure enough that it can't be hacked or bypassed to prevent it from protecting innocent people.

There must also be a reasonable agreement as to who holds the keys to artificial intelligence weapons. Certainly, it can't be the government. They've proven time and again they can't be trusted. Most likely, it would be an independent board consisting of non-partisans who believe in the Second Amendment and the rights of individuals. Even better, when artificial intelligence reaches the level where it is smarter than humans, the artificial intelligence technology will control itself under the restrictions initially established that it must protect the innocent and that it must protect the rights of gun owners.

Yes, it's a tall order with thousands of more things to be worked out, technologically, politically, and socially. But it can be done. After all, when many years ago we set our minds to going to the moon before the end of the 1960s, we were successful. This may be a similarly complex task, but if we decide to do it, it will become a reality.

This essay came about because I was appalled by both the treatment and testimony of Robert Mueller during the congressional coverage

LET'S CALL THE MUELLER HEARINGS WHAT THEY WERE: ELDER ABUSE

Anyone who watched the Mueller hearings for three minutes knows the truth whether they're willing to admit it or not!

An elderly man who might or might not know his own name depending on what time of day you ask him was forced to go through many hours of grueling testimony before the House of Representatives because the Democrats thought they could manipulate him into supporting any lies they told.

Anywhere else except Congress, it would be called "elder abuse."

I can just imagine the planning meeting of a couple of top Democrat House members as they prepared for the hearings:

"Well, Pencil Neck," says one of the ranking members of the Judiciary Committee, "do you think we're going to get enough out of Mueller to impeach the President?"

"Easy, peasy!" chortles Pencil Neck, as giddy as he's ever been. "We can get this guy to say anything. He doesn't even know what planet he's on. We just have to be careful to ask leading questions with "yes" and "no" answers, like: *Isn't it true that you've found evidence that President Trump is an alien from Neptune?* Then, if he hesitates, you say, *All you need to do is say Yes. Thank you for your testimony, sir."*

"But what if he gets confused?," asks the ranking member.

"Of course he's going to be confused," says Pencil Neck. "It's all to our advantage."

"But won't people notice that he's senile?"

"Everyone hates Trump so much that they're not going to notice anything. Before it's over, we'll have testimony from Mueller that Trump practices brain surgery without a license on those he disagrees with."

"Ok, Pencil Neck, if that's what you say."

"And please stop calling me Pencil Neck."

"Why? Everyone else does!"

It's impossible to believe that the ranking Democrats didn't know the physical or mental condition Mueller was in when they subpoenaed him to testify.

They just wanted to use and abuse him to get at the President. Somehow, they thought they could get away with it.

I'm just sorry that after the truth became apparent, one of the Republicans leaders didn't stand up and say: "We have no more questions of Mr. Mueller as we refuse to engage in this blatant example of elder abuse." Nothing more would have needed to be said.

A SKUNK BY ANY OTHER NAME

Just a few days ago, San Francisco had a real problem with crime, drug addicts and juvenile delinquency, among its many other dilemmas.

However the city found a cheap and effective solution to solve those pestering issues.

Now, San Francisco is devoid of felons. There are no more drug addicts on the streets, and delinquency among juveniles has disappeared. And San Francisco's Board of Supervisors, it seems, is overjoyed that it has been able to take on these complex problems and return the city to its former glory.

How did the Supervisors engineer such a seemingly insurmountable task?

It's simple. They passed a resolution saying that felons will no longer be called "felons"; instead, they're now called "justice-involved" persons or "returning residents."

The resolution also makes it clear that there are no more juvenile delinquents. They are now a "young person with justice system involvement," or a "young person impacted by the juvenile justice system."

What about the drug addicts and substance abusers? They're now people "with a history of substance use."

I'm so overjoyed that because of the brainy actions of the San Francisco Board of Supervisors, I can now visit the City by the Bay with no fear of the systemic problem I would have had to deal with only a few days ago.

No felons = no crime! Right?

Let me get off the subject for a minute, then I'll get back to San Francisco.

Many city dwellers in San Francisco and elsewhere may not know that residents of rural and suburban areas over much of the country are having problems with skunks. Yes, the smelly black and white creatures immortalized by Warner Brothers in the Pepé Le Pew cartoons. However, skunk infestations can be a real problem, sometimes even forcing families out of their homes.

Here's my suggestion: there should be a Herculean effort to round up known skunk populations in areas where they're problems. Then the animals can be dropped onto San Francisco's streets.

Immediately, the Board of Supervisors can pass a resolution changing their name to something far more appealing.

It's a win/win situation for everyone. We reduce skunk populations where they're a nuisance or worse, and give them to a city that will welcome them as "precious aromatic animals."

THE DANGER OF EQUALITY

EQUALITY

There's a danger lurking in the House of Representatives.

Actually, there are many dangers in the House, including all 235 democrats. But I'm referring to one in specific.

It's H.R. 5 - The Equality Act.

And if it becomes law, freedom of speech and freedom of religion in America will be gone forever. I'm not exaggerating. That's how serious it is.

The bill was introduced in the House by democrat Rhode Island Rep. David N. Cicilline, and is being co-sponsored by 240 other House members, which includes 3 republicans.

While the bill is quite wordy with plenty of prohibitions on freedom, here's the official summary directly from the official Congressional web site:

This bill prohibits discrimination based on sex, sexual orientation, and gender identity in areas including public accommodations and facilities, education, federal funding, employment, housing, credit, and the jury system. Specifically, the bill defines and includes sex, sexual orientation, and gender identity among the prohibited categories of discrimination or segregation.

The bill expands the definition of public accommodations to include places or establishments that provide (1) exhibitions, recreation, exercise, amusement, gatherings, or displays; (2) goods, services, or programs; and (3) transportation services.

The bill allows the Department of Justice to intervene in equal protection actions in federal court on account of sexual orientation or gender identity.

The bill prohibits an individual from being denied access to a shared facility, including a restroom, a locker room, and a dressing room, that is in accordance with the individual's gender identity.

If you read the entire bill, it does not make exceptions for religious expressions, religious beliefs and the practice of religion. In other words, your pastor or priest will no longer be able to preach that homosexuality is a sin or wrong. The

Colorado cake baker who refused to make a cake for a gay wedding because it violated his religious beliefs would have far fewer legal protections, despite winning his case in the Supreme Court. Under the law, churches and religious institutions would be required to give equal consideration in hiring to homosexuals and transgender people for all positions, including youth counselors, summer camp workers, and even ministers.

And if H.R. 5 becomes law, there will no longer be a need for public restrooms to be designated for men or women. "The bill prohibits an individual from being denied access to a shared facility, including a restroom, a locker room, and a dressing room, that is in accordance with the individual's gender identity." In other words, you can decide if you're feeling more like a man or a woman today in choosing your restroom, locker room, or any other public facility. So, what's the point in putting a gender designation on the door?

If H. R. 5 ever becomes law, you will see many good people fined and/or imprisoned for what was once free speech. The far left will be sure to put the law to the test, just as they did for the Colorado baker, just to see how far they can go in destroying democracy. Lives will be destroyed. The America we once knew as "the land of the free" will be gone forever.

THE FIRST AMENDMENT IS DEAD IN
NEW YORK CITY

"I hate black people, Hispanics, Asians, Native Americans, and everyone else whose skin is not as white as Count Dracula's. I also hate illegal immigrants, and urge you to hate them, too."

The above statement is as offensive as just about any statement every spoken.

However, I support your right to say it, so long as you don't advocate or incite violence or say it in a capacity other than that of your personal opinion. You're allowed your own beliefs, no matter how wrong, or how much I disagree with you. You're also allowed free speech to convince others of your beliefs, even if you're totally wrong. It's in the *First Amendment* of the *United States Constitution* -- which applies to all Americans -- unless you live in New York City.

New York City's Commission on Human Rights has announced that anyone who uses terms such as "illegal alien ... with intent to demean, humiliate or harass a person" is subject to a fine of up to $250,000.

Here's a fact: I think that illegal immigration is wrong and that illegal immigrants are criminals. Can I say that in New York City ? No, not without the city bankrupting me.

Do I hate illegal immigrants? No. But I don't want American taxpayers to pay the bill for the huge tide of illegals who cross the border. Do I want the social problems that inevitably come from such an influx? No, but in the minds of liberals and progressives, this means that I hate every one of them, no matter how much I deny it. I also need to be punished for stating my beliefs. I need to be destroyed, just like Count Dracula needed to be destroyed. New York has assured that a mechanism is in place to accomplish this if I disagree or speak against their progressive policies.

By the way, I will also have to pay a fine of up to $250,000 in New York City if I use a gender pronoun not approved by the person being spoken to or about. So if "he" wants to be called "she" or "it" or something totally absurd, I must comply, or face ruin.

If the NYC Commission on Human Rights is successful at outlawing speech against illegal immigration and the use of your preferred gender pronouns, it will likely start outlawing other speech it finds offensive. Before long, you'll have to watch everything you say. Other societies already have speech police. Is that what we want?

No matter what the penalty, I urge fellow readers to use the words with which you feel comfortable whether in New York City or somewhere else.

When the cases start piling up in the Supreme Court, I believe that the *First Amendment* will be the winner.

If not, all is lost.

AMAZING PREDICTIONS FOR 2020

I was privileged to know and be a good friend of the famous bottle cap collector and supermarket tabloid clairvoyant, Felonius Hornswoggler. He passed away thirty years ago, but if you're old enough, you'll remember that each January he would make startling predictions about what might happen during the upcoming year. And sometimes he would make predictions for the more distant future.

The Internet wasn't around then, so the tabloids were something to entertain you as you waited in line at the supermarket. Those who wrote the headlines were master marketers. A headline from the *Inquiring World News* would jumped out at you: *Clairvoyant Predicts Billy Carter will Cure the Common Cold with Ingredients in Beer and Peanuts!*

Then under the headline was another prediction: *Ronald Regan Will Give Up Politics, Return to the Movies, and Win an Oscar for Best Actor! 100 More Amazing Predictions Inside!*

It was enough to make you pull the tabloid down from the magazine rack and take it home with you.

I'll admit that Felonius' predictions weren't always one hundred percent accurate, but no clairvoyant can see through the fog of the future perfectly.

One day back in March of 1989, I was called to Felonius' bedside. He knew that he only had a couple of days, if not hours, left. It was a sad time, and I knew I had to be there for him. After all, it was the Great Felonius who predicted that I would someday write a best-selling trivia book.

I sat by his bed for a long time, not sure if he was even aware that I was there. The hospital room was dim, but a muted television on the wall displayed the news and gave most of the light.

He opened his eyes, turned to me, and weakly smiled. "I have something for you," he said in a whisper. "Open that drawer by the bed and you'll find an envelope. Pull it out, but don't open it."

I did as Felonius asked. My name was on the envelope.

"I've made predictions about the future," he explained. "Nothing is written in stone, but I've never been able to see more clearly. I saw what the world will be like in the year 2020. It was as if I were watching it on TV." He was very weak, but obviously very excited.

"I'm entrusting this to you. Don't open it until thirty years from today. Then you can decide if you want to release it to the world. It will be your decision."

Then he closed his eyes and faded away before me.

Despite the temptation, the envelope remained sealed until yesterday, the 30th anniversary of Felonius' passing. As I pulled out the paper and unfolded it, my hands were trembling. And as I began to read, I was amazed and frightened by ten predictions.

Here is what the paper said in its entirety:

PREDICTIONS FOR THE YEAR 2020 BY FELONIUS HORNSWOGGLER

1. A politician known as AOC will become the savior of the land. Citizens will vote to repeal the constitution and name her Supreme Ruler of the World for Life.
2. Cows will become extinct.
3. Obesity will disappear as the government takes control of all meal menus and provides everyone with a weekly ration of tofu and spinach.
4. All houses will be topped by windmills.

5. Automobiles will become obsolete as everyone walks or rides bicycles. Airplanes will also disappear and be replaced by wind-powered ships for most international travel.
6. Health care will be provided free to everyone and will become so popular that waiting lists will be up to 20 years long.
7. Those who don't want to work will be honored with a national holiday.
8. Congress will pass a law requiring Senators and Representatives to smoke marijuana before debating legislation.
9. Climate change deniers will be rounded up and sent to Kim Jong-un for target practice on his missile ranges.
10. Fox News Channel will apologize for all its lies and go off the air.

I was, of course, stunned. The Great Felonius had predicted the rise of AOC, even before she was born.

There is only one year before all this comes true, according to Felonius. My mind went into overdrive: should I put lots of hamburger meat and steaks in the freezer now, before it's too late? Should I buy more freezers and tons of hamburger and steak? Would the windmills provide enough energy to power the freezers? What will I do when cows become extinct?

Then, I remembered the television in the hospital room those thirty years ago, and I understood. The TV channel had been set to CNN.

Somehow, Felonius had failed to tune in to the real future of 2020. Instead, by whatever means of divination, he had channeled the CNN newsroom of 2020, along with the hopes and dreams of its reporters, anchors, and producers!

As long as we are aware of our possible futures, we can change them. Felonius saw a possible future, one in which AOC is the person who decides how the rest of us will live, tofu and all!

Fortunately, as long as conservatives are still in the picture, we can make a future that we understand, one of patriotism, individualism, and a love for burgers!

By the way, why has Alexandria Ocasio-Cortez taken control of the Democrat party?

THE ART OF A WINK AND THE DEAL

I almost got kicked off my trivia team Saturday night! I arrived at the Elks Lodge early to find three of my teammates already at our table. I said "hi" and sat down by Sonny as everyone acknowledged me and continued their animated conversation.

The first sentence I heard was "...And they said on TV that Trump has lied more than seven thousand times since he was elected." The other two agreed, and then they were off to criticize the President's performance at the summit in Vietnam. "Can you believe that he says he likes Kim Jong-Un?" Sonny said. "I mean why doesn't he call him out for being the killer he is? Why doesn't he call him on the human rights violations and starving his own people!" My other teammates were in fast agreement and making similar statements.

Sonny then turned to me and said, "Hey, sorry, we didn't mean to leave you out of the conversation."

"Don't worry, that's okay," I said, "I came in on it late."

"It's just you were so quiet. You do agree with us, don't you?" he asked me, looking me right in the eyes.

"No," I answered.

His jaw dropped. I think he was stunned.

"The President's purpose in going to the summit was to work toward getting an agreement to denuclearize North Korea," I said. "The President is trying to prevent a war. I don't think it's likely that he can ever get an agreement if he goes into the meeting telling Kim Jong-un how horrible he is."

"Well, maybe if he had done that he would have shamed him into an agreement. He certainly didn't get anything done by playing Mr. Nice Guy!"

I nodded. "As the President said, 'You have to be willing to walk away from a deal if it's not a good one.'"

Sonny challenged me as the two teammates looked on, "You didn't vote for him, did you?"

"Yes," I said. "Sonny, you have to understand that not everyone agrees with you. There are conservatives in the world!"

He was shaking his head. "But, I've known you for twenty years..."

To make a long story short, I didn't get kicked off the team, but the next two and a half hours felt pretty icy. Despite the fact that I usually have the winning answers on the team (yes, I'm a best-selling trivia book author), I didn't feel very welcome.

If Sonny had been interested in having a real conversation, he would have learned that I agree with him: Little Rocket Man really is a cold blooded killer, but there's a lot more to it than that.

Analysis

If you were watching Fox News on Saturday morning, you saw President Trump speaking for over two hours at the CPAC about everything from the witch hunt and the economy, to the wall, and North Korea. On the other hand, if you were watching CNN or MSNBC, you saw "Feel the Bern" Bernie talking about his socialist "solutions" for this country.

However, for whatever reason, my TV was tuned to Fox News. And sure enough, toward the end of his mostly off-the-cuff speech, President Trump addressed the summit and Jim Jong-un, saying that he and the dictator like each other and have a good relationship, despite the fact he had to walk away from the summit because the deal wasn't right for the U.S.

Let's address the question directly: How can the President like and have a good relationship with a cold blooded murderer?

Answer: The President has been left with a big problem. The ineptitude of previous Presidents has left him in a difficult situation. Either he reaches a solution, or the Korean War starts up again. With the resurgence of the war, there will be hundreds of thousands, if not millions of deaths.

So the President is looking for a deal. In this deal, the North Koreans give up their nuclear and intercontinental ballistic missile (ICBM) programs. Little Rocket Man avoids death, and has the opportunity to bring his country into this century.

So what if the President walks into the meeting room at the summit, points his finger at the dictator, and screams, "You're a dirty, murdering piece of scum and deserve to die. Let's make a deal!"

Somehow, I don't think the deal gets made.

But the President is a businessman. He knows that in order to get a deal, the other person must be made to feel important. So he metaphorically walks into the conference room with a clothes pin attached to his nose, and treats his opponent with undeserved respect and kindness. It's not what he wants to do, but eventually getting a deal means that he has to resort to making Little Rocket Man feel good about himself.

Little Rocket Man does the logical thing. He says there's no deal unless the U.S. releases all of the sanctions and lets him keep a good deal of his nuclear program. President Obama gave in to Iran with everything the Mullahs wanted, so why shouldn't President Trump give in? After all, it looks really bad to walk away from a summit without a deal. Surely, the President doesn't want to subject himself to that embarrassment!

Well, unfortunately for Little Rocket Man, the President wrote a book called *The Art of the Deal*. He knows that you can walk away!

But when he gets back to the U.S. and the CPAC, why does President Trump talk about his good relationship with Little Rocket Man? He's back in the U.S., so why doesn't he call him a killer and absolute scum?

The answer is simple. More negotiations are yet to come and he can't say one thing here and another thing there without crashing the deal.

So, when the President talks about how much he likes the Rocket Man, it's like he's giving you a wink. The wink is implied, not real, but it lets the audience know that the President knows what he's doing, despite all appearances. Just play along. You're supposed to understand that this is part of the negotiation process, not a perfect view of reality. Unfortunately, liberals don't see the wink. I don't think they ever see the wink.

But eventually there will be a deal. The Korean War will end and North Korea will eventually become a part of the world community.

It's all because our President knows how to wink.

'SHE' IS WORTH FIGHTING FOR!

She is the biggest ship, me lads, that ever sailed the sea.
*As graceful as a swan **she** goes; we sail **her** at our ease.*
From Arabie around Cape Hope we proudly make our
way,
To keep all Europe movin' from our base at Bantry Bay!

**-- From *Bringing Home the Oil* by The Clancy Brothers and
Tommy Makum in a 1960's Gulf Oil commercial.**

"She" is about to disappear due to political correctness. Scotland's National Newspaper, *The Scotsman* is reporting that the Scottish Maritime Museum is giving in to political correctness and will no longer refer to ships as "she." The newspaper, quoting the museum's director, David Mann, says that a vandal has been successful in helping the museum make it's decision:

"For the second time this year, the museum has been targeted by a vandal, who has destroyed one of the interpretation signs which follow the universally adopted and centuries old maritime tradition of referring to vessels as female.

Like other maritime museums and institutions, we *recognise* the changes in society and are committed to introducing gender neutral interpretation."

Here's my question: Why doesn't the museum stand up to the vandal? Why doesn't it set up surveillance, arrest and prosecute the person doing this? Giving in this easily to a politically correct vandal sends a message to other politically correct vandals: *Go ahead and vandalize. You'll win. They'll give in.*

And isn't it the job of a museum to preserve history and tradition?

Why doesn't the museum say, "We will stand up for centuries of sailors and sailing?"

"She" is worth fighting for!

Note: The word "recognize" is spelled "recognise," as is correct in Britain. Since it falls within a quotation, I did not change it.

A REALLY INCONVENIENT TRUTH

You probably missed this important story on the nightly news, or on the front page of your local newspaper.

Why?

Because it's not there.

It's really inconvenient for the liberal media to tell you about the *Jakobshavn Isbrae* glacier in Greenland. It's inconvenient because the glacier is no longer melting. In fact, it's been growing significantly again for the past two years, after melting for the previous twenty.

The article in *Nature Geoscience* attributes the glacier's growth to cooling of the ocean waters around it. According to the abstract: "Observations and modelling trace the origins of this cooling to anomalous wintertime heat loss in the boundary current that circulates around the southern half of Greenland."

This is one of the very important glaciers that scientists have been closely watching for decades. They've offered it, time after time, as proof of global warming.

Yes, it's really inconvenient for the media, and yes, if they report on it at all, they will claim it is an anomaly that means nothing. In other words, they'll only report the news that fits their narrative and ignore the rest.

What do you think? Will Al Gore mention this in his next book? Or is it possible he'll get on his large-carbon-footprint private jet to check it out for himself before being embarrassed into giving back his Nobel Peace Prize and admitting he was wrong?

Sorry, I forgot. He can't admit he was wrong. He's a liberal!

WHEN GREEN IS ACTUALLY RED

If you're old enough to remember the Soviet Union, or if you've studied socialism or communism, you know that the color red is associated with tyranny, despotism, and government control of everyday life. It's associated with lies, violence, intimidation, and manipulation as a method of controlling the populace.

No, I'm not talking about the "red states" or "blue states" that media use to refer to Republican (red) or Democrat (blue) dominated areas. I'm talking about an earlier time in history when "red" was synonymous with a total loss of independence, a surrender to absolute government control. It's a reference to the red flag of the former Soviet Union.

In a communist system, everyone except the power elite, lives in poverty and does what he or she is told, or else suffers the consequences (usually not very pleasant: Can you say "Gulag?" Can you say "Venezuela?")

In a capitalist system, most of those willing to work, live in the "middle class," with the opportunity to make decisions and take actions that will move them up or down the economic ladder, depending on their capabilities and decisions.

Unfortunately, school kids these days don't study history. They're not aware of what happened in Russia in 1917. They don't know about the "Red Scare" of the 1950s, or being taught to hide under school desks in order to survive a nuclear war. They don't know why Cuba is desperately poor, rather than rich, as it was before 1959. And they don't understand why the "Green New Deal" is actually the Red New Deal.

If you sign on to the Green New Deal, you're actually signing on to a "Red Deal."

The Green New Deal requires that we allow government to control our lives. The government will spend trillions of dollars and take control of all aspects of our lives to ensure that everyone has the basic necessities, while trying to control the weather by throwing us back into the stone age. Actually, the progressive elite will live in luxury, but you'll be among those waiting in bread lines, when and if bread is available.

Here's the progressive argument for why we must agree to the Green New Deal: ALL climate scientists agree with AOC that the world will end in twelve years unless we act now! Not even one disagrees! It's REALLY, REALLY BAD! We must give up all of our freedoms because of the reckless climate decisions make by those who came before us. If you don't agree with this, the world will end in 2031! There's no time for debate or further study, just agree with the progressives and let them take control of the world. You must do it RIGHT NOW! Every minute you wait is a minute closer to the end of the world!

Here's the conservative argument against the Green New Deal: Socialists and communists LIE to us to take away our freedoms. While climate is actually changing, as it has been over the past few billion years, there is no definitive evidence that humans are causing climate change, or that we can do anything about it. However, there is proof that scientists have been cooking the data to make the case for their climate claims and theories. While we must monitor and debate climate change and all other issues pertaining to our society, we must act with caution and make decisions based on deliberate and thoughtful considerations.

Unfortunately, progressives have hijacked climate change as a way to take away your freedoms: "Give us absolute control NOW, or we'll all be dead by 2031! REALLY! YOU MUST DO IT RIGHT NOW!"

Here's my advice. Don't be afraid for the polar bears. Be afraid of losing your freedoms!

Green actually means "Red" in the worst sort of way.

A NEW WORD FOR 'LIBERALS'

Let's face it, liberals are good with the use of the English language. The term "pro-choice" is much more palatable than "pro-abortion." They say "undocumented immigrant" rather than "illegal alien." And "immigration reform" really means you want open borders.

"Income inequality" means that they want to take my money and give it other people.

The "Green New Deal" means that they want us to become a socialist country and throw out the window every American value we've every known.

If you disagree with them on spending hundreds of billions of dollars to slow down climate change, you are a "climate change denier." "Climate change denier" makes you sound like you must be an absolute moron because you deny what to them is such an obvious scientific truth. Everyone else in the world understands this, so why don't you, you evil conservative!

All of these euphemisms got me to thinking about all of the obvious truths that liberals deny!

They now want to be known as "progressives" because the term "liberal" has become a bit tarnished over the past several years. However, my suggestion is that we all start referring to them as "reality deniers."

The reality is that the economy is booming due to favorable taxes, less regulation, and optimistic consumers. Liberals deny it, saying they will improve the economy by raising taxes, raising the minimum wage, and guaranteeing a minimum income, even for those unwilling to work.

The reality is that evil people attacked the United States on 9-11 because they hated the U.S., our beliefs, and all Americans. Liberals deny it saying that 9-11 and similar terrorism are reactions to America's aggressive and arrogant foreign policy. If

America would just leave them alone, they would leave us alone.

The reality is that Hillary, despite her unparalleled skill at wiping servers with a big lint-free cloth, really was a horrible candidate and deserved to lose! Liberals don't so much deny it. Instead they pretend that she never existed.

I don't have to create a long list of all the obvious truths that liberals deny because you're already familiar with them.

But one thing is certain, it's time to start calling liberals what they are: "Reality Deniers!"

ODDS AND ENDS YOU MISSED IN THE NEWS

If you're reading an American newspaper, or watching *CNN, MSNBC,* or even *Fox News,* you're missing news even more important than which mean message one politician just tweeted about another.

Liberals want to take away our freedom of speech and the right to bear arms. In Europe, they're far ahead of the United States in taking away liberties. Here are a few examples of how these left wing policies are impacting Europe in a negative way:

- The Swedish government is working to ban runes, the ancient alphabet of the Vikings. The government reasons that because the Nazis used runes in some of its symbology during World War Two, the alphabet represents racism, hate and evil. If this ban takes place, ancient archaeological monuments will be covered or destroyed and runes will no longer be used in jewelry, art, or other forms of expression. Many Swedes believe this is an assault on their cultural heritage in favor of refugees who are flooding the country. Hundreds of people are being prosecuted in Sweden for simply speaking out against the mass immigration of Islamic refugees. In Sweden, to say you oppose the acceptance of refugees is considered "hate speech" and is a crime.
- London has accepted multiculturalism to the extent that comedian John Cleese of Monty Python fame says that London "isn't a British city anymore."
- Seville, Spain is welcoming the construction of the first mosque to be built there in 700 years. Like much of Europe, Spain is welcoming Islamic refugees without regard to the consequences of accepting people who are culturally different, and who refuse to assimilate into the culture of the country to which they come.
- A survey by a German research institute finds that only around 20 per cent of Germans feel that they are able to express their opinions in public, especially when the

subject of speech is about refugees or Islam. Seventy-five percent of Germans are against the ban of classic children's literature like Pippi Lonstocking. The bans are taking place because such works are politically incorrect and don't represent today's multiculturalism.

- In France, there are as many practicing Muslims as Catholics in the 18 to 29 year-old demographic. It has been proposed that a minaret (a Muslim prayer tower) be added to Notre Dame Cathedral during the promised reconstruction.

Maybe the few bullet points above will give you a feel for what is going on in Europe. The liberal American press certainly isn't going to mention it to you.

It's Europe now; it could be the United States in a few years.

GO, COACH JOE!

Imagine that Joe Biden is a football coach, rather than a politician. And he's the chief coach for one of the great teams.

It's just a few days before the big game. Coach Joe walks behind his team, taking time to bend over and smell the hair of the lineup as he goes. Eventually, after several deep inhales, he works his way to the front.

"Hey, guys," he says, standing directly before them, "It's time to get ready for the big game."

"Go! Go! Go!," the team enthusiastically chants in response, throwing their fists into the air.

"And by the way," advises Coach Joe, "be sure to ask Smith about that conditioner he's using. I could sniff it all day."

The team pauses their chant for a moment, looking at each other in momentary confusion. But in a few seconds, they continue, even more excitedly. "Go! Go! Fight! Fight! Win! Win," they scream.

Coach Joe holds his hands up in response, open palms facing his team. "Hey, team, don't get too excited. You know, the Chinese team we're about to play are a bunch of amateurs. They're no competition for us. So, I'm cancelling practice until after the game."

The team becomes silent and seems a bit downcast.

"Hey, guys," he says. "The Chinese team is just like the Russian team. We don't have anything to worry about. Take some time and relax."

One of the smaller guys in the middle of the lineup raises his hand.

"Yes," acknowledges the coach.

Timidly, the little guy says, "But, maybe we should run some plays, just to be sure we're prepared."

"Thanks for offering your opinion," the Coach says with a big toothy grin. "You know, I love to hear other viewpoints. Really, really, I do. But I'm not here to waste our time with something as crazy as worrying about the Chinese."

The little guy holds his eyes down in shame for making such a stupid statement. The quarterback, standing next to the little guy, puts an arm around his teammate's shoulder in a supportive way.

Then Coach Joe says. "You know, I'm a little sleepy. I think I'm going home to take a nap. Maybe you guys should, too."

Go, Coach Joe! Go and take a nap.

CAN NOTRE DAME BE SAVED FROM ARCHITECTS, POLITICANS AND POLITICAL CORRECTNESS?

French President Macron has promised that *Notre Dame* Cathedral will be rebuilt in only five years and "even more beautifully" than before.

Already, billions of Euros have been pledged by the extremely wealthy.

And a design contest is already under way.

What does a design contest mean?

It means that restoring the building to the Gothic masterpiece that it was is not an option. Architects will vie for the opportunity to showcase their modern reinterpretation in the most showy and extravagant, all-inclusive ways possible. No longer will it be a Catholic or Christian cathedral, as many are arguing that it should be secular and not a showcase for religion.

In *Domus*, an architecture and design magazine, Architect Tom Wilkinson observes that President Macron's desire for a more beautiful building "...raises as many questions as it answers. By whose standards of beauty?" He then argues that Notre Dame might better be a "monument to truth, rather than beauty." Under that scenario, the truth could be political truth. Here's the danger that Wilkinson sees:

"To rebuild 'even more beautifully' in this regard could mean, for instance, transforming Notre-Dame into a memorial to the generations of peasants who were exploited to fund it, and the heretics murdered by its client. Or, if the barbarism of which this building is a document has grown too cold to trouble us, why not a monument to a more up-to-date form of political truth? How about, in this instance, a monument to *le gilet jaune inconnu [translation: unknown yellow vest,* Ed., Mr. Evil], complete with a dayglow spire? Or if that seems a little frivolous, what about the approximately 100 Algerians who were killed by the French police while protesting the Algerian War in 1961, many of them thrown into the Seine at the foot of Notre-

Dame? These victims of the state could be memorialized by replacing Viollet-le-Duc's flèche with – why not? – a graceful minaret." **-- Tom Wilkinson** in ***Domus***

While others in the media are quoting Wilkinson as promoting a minaret, I think this is his dry way of warning what a can of worms a liberal reinterpretation of *Notre Dame* might come to. Or he might be serious. His editorial style leaves one to wonder, but once you start making changes and reinterpretations, where do you stop? Maybe you just go wild and show your flair for modern design and whatever is on your political mind. After all, you've got billions of Euros to play with and liberal politicians who will let you get away with it.

Notre Dame is a Christian monument and should remain so. It should be restored to it's Gothic splendor without making politically correct accommodations to Muslims, Buddhist, atheists and others.

I'm certainly no great architect like Mr. Wilkinson. However, for those who think the addition of a minaret is appropriate, let me suggest some equally sane and equally appropriate architectural ideas:

- Add graceful giant golden arches and a drive-thru.
- Add a graceful giant statue of Colonel Sanders, holding a chicken leg in one hand and a French baguette in the other to

symbolize the acceptance of both French and American cuisine.

- Build a graceful megalithic nose sculpture to celebrate French snobbery toward Americans (you know, the same Americans who saved them from Nazism in WWII).

If we can't have the real *Notre Dame*, I would much rather see the golden arches there instead of a minaret!

FINAL THOUGHTS FROM A CONSERVATIVE VAMPIRE

If you're like my wife, this is the first chapter of the book you're reading, since she always jumps to the last chapter to see how it ends. However, if you're a normal human being, like most people, you've read a few dozen short essays from the viewpoint of a proud conservative.

As this book is about to go to press, there is much going on in the news. The Democrats are trying to impeach the President over the phone call to the Ukrainian president. Deluded Hillary is talking about jumping into the Presidential race because all of the other Democrats running are losers and can't beat Donald Trump. (Special note to President Trump: You're the best at making up nicknames for your opponents. However, let me offer you this one. If Hillary runs again, you've already used "Crooked Hillary." How about: "Deluded Hillary" this time?) Also in the news: AOC now wants to create a "Just Society" by putting the U.S. in hundreds of trillions of dollars more in debt than she's already proposed with the Green New Deal and Medicare For All. (By the way, after trillions comes quadrillions.)

Despite all of the negative and fake news, I am optimistic for the future of this country. There is no doubt that if the progressives win the 2020 presidential election, the United States will fall into a tailspin that will ensure a societal crash and burn. However, I believe that Bernie, Pocahontas, Beto, and the others have set themselves up for failure with extreme beliefs that fall so far out of the mainstream that election to the highest office in the land is beyond comprehension.

And I understand that you might or might not like President Trump. He can certainly be egocentric, abrasive and crude at times, and he doesn't understand the rules of how to be a traditional politician. The nicknames he throws at his opponents may or may not be fair, but they stick, as

Pencil Neck and Pocahontas can tell you! On the other hand, the President has an irreverent sense of humor that leaves some bent over in laughter and others cringing.

A recent Fox News poll shows that fifty-one percent of Americans want President Trump impeached and removed from office. However, back to the theme of "the conservative vampire," I expect that many of those being polled are simply afraid to express their support for the President. Instead of saying what they think, they protect themselves by telling the pollster what he or she (or other gender pronoun) wants to hear.

So even if you dislike the President immensely, on election day are you going to ignore the booming economy, low unemployment rate for everyone (including minorities), safer borders, safer cities, or the rebuilding of our military?

I hope not.

Unlike the great supermarket tabloid clairvoyant Felonius Hornswoggler, I cannot predict the future. However, I don't believe you have to be psychic to foresee a favorable and prosperous future for the United States, especially if conservatives can overcome the dangerous progressive agenda being thrown out by the Democratic party.

For the most part, Americans are smart people. They are looking for an alternative to the traditional politics and politicians of big talk and no action. As the old joke goes: *When all was said and done, more was said than done.*

I believe people really do want the swamp drained.

However, there are big pockets of worry for this country. As this book is about to go to press, a new poll conducted by YouGov, a reputable polling firm, shows that young people are embracing socialism as never before. According to the *Washington Examiner*:

"The results are downright disturbing. The new data show that 64% of Gen Z and 70% of millennials say they're likely to vote for a socialist. Meanwhile, 20% of millennials think the *Communist Manifesto* "better guarantees freedom and equality" than the Declaration of Independence."

Thankfully, young people often come to their senses as they gain age and experience. As Winston Churchill is famously erroneously quoted: "If you're not a liberal when you're twenty, you don't have a heart. If you're not a conservative when you're forty, you don't have a brain." (It was actually President John Adams who said it, or a version thereof.)

Additionally, as I go to press, Beto has just dropped out of the presidential election and Michael Bloomberg seems ready to get in. Jeff Sessions is asking Alabama voters to give him back his old Senate job. Even *Saturday Night Live* is making fun of Pocahontas and her $52 Trillion Medicare For All plan (you know, the one that won't raise your taxes). Liberal politicians and media refuse to congratulate President Trump on the military mission that killed Isis leader Abu Bakr al-Baghdadi, barely acknowledging it happened. And Democrats in Washington are shaking in their boots just before the Inspector General's report reveals the truth about the Foreign Intelligence Surveillance Act abuses by the Justice Department and the FBI. (I won't be surprised if it eventually comes out that orders for the illegal use of FISA documents to frame Donald Trump came from the highest levels of the Obama Whitehouse).

Impeachment is looming for President Trump. There's little doubt that no significant legislation will be passed before the election because the Democrats refuse to give the President a win, even if it's good for the United States. Partisanship on trade agreements, immigration, and myriad other issues, is beyond reason. The Democrats (and some Republicans) are so afraid that the swamp will be drained that they see the real possibility of losing their ill-earned power. In the end, the President will win the impeachment trial, and will very likely make a big impact on drying out the swap. Also, I believe that you can expect an ever improving economy over the next several years, a decrease in terrorism as the U.S. gets even tougher on radical extremism, and a resurgence of American pride.

As for me, I shall anonymously remain in the shadows like a good conservative vampire. My essays and commentaries on subjects of interest to other concerned Americans will continue to appear in my blog: *ConservativesAreEvil.com*. And when I have amassed another substantial body of work, you can expect *The Conservative Vampire, Volume Two*.

Until then, I encourage you to keep up with what is going on in the world and examine the news with a somewhat skeptical eye. Realize that your freedoms and liberties are at stake if those who don't care about your values are elected.

Pass this book along to a liberal friend, if you dare. Maybe you will convert him or her to your more conservative viewpoints. If not, it will give you subject matter and ammunition to debate those progressive ideas.

Also pass this book along to your conservative friends who also hide in the shadows, afraid of their liberal "friends." They will not only appreciate it, they will understand.

--Mr. Evil

APPENDIX

It is my intention to provide sources for much of the information that appears in this book, starting with the cover. While much of the material is opinion and is based on general knowledge, a good portion is commentary on news broadcasts, online articles, or other media information. When possible, I will provide whatever source I have available, although in some cases, it may be incomplete or secondary. Also, please be aware the URLs (web addresses) given were correct at the time of publication, but may have changed or become unavailable at a later time.

The Conservative Vampire book cover:
I designed the cover using graphics from pixabay.com. The vampire shown on the front cover

is a representation of Graf Orlok, the Dracula character from the silent 1922 German film *Nosferatu*. The title role was played by actor Max Schreck.

All other graphics in this book: All graphics and images in this book are direct images, composites, or adaptations of images found on pixabay.com.

Introduction: The term "conservatives are evil" comes from a column by Dr. Charles Krauthammer originally published in the *Washington Post* on July 26, 2002: *Conservatives Can Agree That Liberals Are Stupid*. The quote in it's entirety is: "To understand the workings of American politics, you have to understand this fundamental law: Conservatives think liberals are stupid. Liberals think conservatives are evil."

The Conservative Vampire: I make references to Roddy McDowell (1938 – 1998) and Darin McGavin (1922 – 2006). Roddy McDowall was an English actor who, as a child, starred in films such as *How Green Was My Valley* (1941) and *My Friend Flicka* (1943). As an adult, he is probably best remembered as Cornelius in the original *Planet of the Apes* (1968) film. For the purpose of this book, the mention of Roddy McDowall is a reference to his role as Peter Vincent in the 1985 vampire film *Fright Night*. He played a television actor in a horror series who is recruited by a teenager to help dispatch a real vampire who has moved into the neighborhood.

Darin McGavin is probably best remembered as the father in *A Christmas Story* (1983). You may remember him, however, as newspaper reporter Karl Kolchak, from the TV movies *The Night Stalker* (1972) and *The Night Strangler* (1973), two of the highest rated TV movies ever at that time. The movies led the way to a television series *Kolchak: The Night Stalker* in 1974 and 1975, in which McGavin reprised the role, now set in Chicago, as a reporter working for the Independent News Service who tracks down supernatural creatures. In one episode, Kolchak recruits the services of a rabbi to help him defeat a golum, a monster made of mud from Jewish folklore.

Forgive Me, Pastor, But My Heroes Have Always Been Cowboys: The song *My Heroes Have Always Been Cowboys* was written by Sharon Vaughn and first recorded by Waylon Jennings in 1976. Willie Nelson recorder it as part of the soundtrack to the Robert Redford and Jane Fonda film *The Electric Horseman* (1979.)

Gene Autry (1907 – 1998), Roy Rogers (1911 – 1998), and Tex Ritter (1905 – 1974) were all hugely popular movie starts in American western movies. *Hopalong Cassidy*, *Gunsmoke*, and *The Cisco Kid* were popular western programs during the golden age of radio. All of the programs also had lives in television and film.

There's A Reason for the Fireworks: The article is based on general historical knowledge, and makes no references to specific sources.

They Deserve It, But...: The essay is based on numerous articles and sources which reported that the President was considering locating illegal immigrants in sanctuary cities. This *New York Times* article by Eileen Sullivan from April 12, 2019 is an excellent example of the coverage: *Trump Says He Is Considering Releasing Migrants in 'Sanctuary Cities':* (https://www.nytimes.com/2019/04/12/us/politics/trump-sanctuary-cities.html).

A Cold-Hearted Republican: No specific sources are referenced.

OZ: An Interesting Place to Visit: All references are to the classic 1939 MGM film *The Wizard of Oz*. The film is based on the children's fantasy novel *The Wonderful Wizard of Oz* (1900) by L. Frank Baum.

My Wife's Calendar: No specific sources are referenced.

Welcome To My Hate-Filled Home: The essay references multiple articles in which Elizabeth Warren is quoted as refusing to do a town hall meeting on Fox News because the network is a "hate for profit racquet." This *New York Times* article is from May 14, 1019: *Warren Calls Fox News a 'Hate-for-Profit Racket' and Refuses an Appearance:* (https://www.nytimes.com/2019/05/14/us/politics/elizabeth-warren-fox-news.html).

The nickname, Pocahontas, President Trump often uses in reference to Elizabeth Warren and her false claim of Native American heritage, is based on an actual person. A fanciful animated Disney movie loosely based on the character Pocahontas came out in 1995. Here is the Wikipedia reference to the real 17th century Native American: (https://en.wikipedia.org/wiki/Pocahontas).

It's a Mad Mad Mad Mad World: The title of this chapter refers to a madcap comedy film from 1963. However, the gist of the essay is based on articles from The *Voice of Europe* website:

91-year-old Swede prosecuted and heavily fined for stating that Muslims "seem to be inbred": (https://voiceofeurope.com/2019/04/91-year-old-swede-prosecuted-and-heavily-fined-for-stating-that-muslims-seem-to-be-inbred/).

Swedish journalist suspended from Facebook for mentioning Tommy Robinson, and stating that we should accept others' opinions even if we don't agree with them: (https://voiceofeurope.com/2019/03/swedish-journalist-suspended-from-facebook-for-mentioning-tommy-robinson-and-stating-that-we-should-accept-others-opinions-even-if-we-dont-agree-with-them/).

Numerous media sources covered Christiane Amanpour's interview with James Comey in which she asked if Trump supporters should be "shut down" for hate speech. This article is from Fox News: *CNN's Christiane Amanpour asks Comey if FBI should have shut down 'hate speech' from Trump rallies:* (https://www.foxnews.com/entertainment/cnns-christiane-amanpour-asks-comey-if-fbi-should-have-shut-down-hate-speech-from-trump-rallies).

Married With Children: This essay is based on an article by CC Pecknold in the *Catholic Herald*: *The West can learn a lot from Hungary's pro-family policies:* (https://catholicherald.co.uk/dailyherald/2019/04/25/the-west-can-learn-a-lot-from-hungarys-pro-family-policies/).

The New York Times survey article is: *Americans Are Having Fewer Babies. They Told Us Why:* (https://www.nytimes.com/2018/07/05/upshot/americans-are-having-fewer-babies-they-told-us-why.html).

Where Have All the Conservatives Gone: No specific references are made.

My Great Great Great Great Great Grandfather Says He's Sorry. But He Doesn't Mean It Because He's Dead!!!: Many news sources reported Mexico's President calling on the Pope and Spain to apologize for the conquest of

America. This report is from the Associated Press: *Mexico president asks Spain, Pope to apologize for conquest:* (https://www.apnews.com/38e67278ad88472f8b59f0 50546fd45e).

The Return of Judas: According to the *Bible*, Judas Iscariot was one of the twelve apostles, and the one who sold out Jesus for crucifixion. His name is used in this essay as a metaphor for the betrayal of Christians by a small Italian town near Bologna. *Russia Today* is the source for this article *'Beyond fanaticism': Crosses in Italian cemetery covered to avoid offending other religions:* (https://www.rt.com/news/456057-italy-church-hides-crosses-offends/).

How to Tell When A Conservative is in the Room: No specific references are made.

What You Win Prizes For In Europe: The *Deutsche Welle* article can be found at: (https://www.dw.com/en/antonio-guterres-the-uns-utopian-guardian-and-cosmopolitan/a-48972000).

The Voice of America article is at: (https://voiceofeurope.com/2019/06/open-borders-are-the-source-of-europes-strength-says-the-un-secretary-general/).

A Matter of Trust: If you ask Amazon's Alexa: *"Alexa, who is the worse President in History?"* you will get the answer:

"Here's something I found on WorldAtlas.com: In the 2018 APSA rankings, Donald Trump held the distinction of the number one worst American president. Donald Trump has been criticized for inconsistent policies, a lack of experience, the cutting of funding for social services, discriminatory immigration policies and more.

An article from Politico about the APSA poll can be found here: (https://www.politico.com/story/2018/02/19/presidential-rankings-survey-trump-417103).

Why Refugees Keep Coming: The website quoted is the official online presence of the Hungarian government: (https://www.kormany.hu/en/news/over-1-55-billion-euros-has-been-spent-on-the-migrant-cards).

My Psychic Wife: The 91st Academy Awards (Oscars), presented by the Academy of Motion Picture Arts and Sciences, occurred at the Dolby Theatre in Hollywood, California on February 24, 2019. They were seen on the ABC television network.

Carnac the Magnificent was a great mystic seer from the East, played by Johnny Carson on the Tonight Show in many episodes of the talk/comedy program between 1964 and 1992.

Trump Vs. Jesus: The opinion article cited comes from the *Dallas Morning News* and can be found here: (https://www.dallasnews.com/opinion/commentary/2016/11/06/10-reasons-you-cant-be-a-christian-and-vote-for-donald-trump/).

A link to the article from the *Investor's Business Daily* about fact checkers can be found at: (https://www.investors.com/politics/editorials/fact-checkers-big-media/).

How You Can Make TV Commercials Even Worse: Codes and rulings of the UK's Advertising Standards Authority can be found here: (https://www.asa.org.uk/codes-and-rulings/advertising-codes/non-broadcast-code.html).

A Modest Proposal For Ending Gun Violence and Saving the Second Amendment: No specific articles or sources are referenced. The essay is an opinion piece based on general news coverage of gun violence and mass shootings over the past several years.

Let's Call the Mueller Hearings What They Were: Elder Abuse!: Robert Mueller testified before the U.S. House of Representatives on July 24, 2019. I was carried on multiple broadcast outlets, and widely reported in other media.

The nickname "Pencil Neck" given to Representative Adam Schiff by President Trump, while fitting, is not original. The first use I can find of the name "Pencil Neck" comes from wrestling legend "Classy" Freddie Blassie (1918 – 2003), who used it in reference to a carnival performer who supposedly had a neck "like a stack of dimes." More recently and more famously, in the movie *Ghost Busters* (1984), Dr. Peter Venkman (Bill Murray) uses "Pencil Neck" as a name to insult Environmental Protection Agency bad guy Walter

Peck (William Atherton) just before Peck shuts down the containment grid and causes paranormal chaos throughout New York City.

A Skunk By Any Other Name: The decision to sanitize language in San Francisco was reported by many sources, including *Fox News*: (https://www.foxnews.com/politics/san-francisco-board-adopts-new-language-for-criminals-turning-convicted-felon-into-justice-involved-person).

The Danger of Equality: The entire text of H.R. 5 can be found on the official U.S. Congress website: (https://www.congress.gov/bill/116th-congress/house-bill/5/text).

The First Amendment is Dead in New York City: The entire body of New York City's human rights laws can be found on its official website: (https://www1.nyc.gov/site/cchr/law/text-of-the-law.page).

An article on Fox News summarizing the law is at: (https://www.foxnews.com/us/new-york-city-250g-illegal-alien-immigration).

Amazing Predictions For 2020: This essay is a fantasy article and references general news from multiple sources, but no specific references are cited.

The Art of a Wink and the Deal: The chapter title is a play on the title of Donald Trump's best-seller *The Art of the Deal*. The article references television coverage of various events on Fox News, CNN and MSNBC from March 2, 2019.

"She" Is Worth Fighting For!: The song *Bringing Home The Oil* is by The Clancy Brothers and Tommy Makum. It was used in a 1960's Gulf Oil commercial. If I remember correctly, it was a commercial that aired during the *NBC Nightly News*, and probably also on other programs. The commercial can be seen on *YouTube* at: (https://www.youtube.com/watch?v=yAFMgt4FeK0 &feature=youtu.be).

The article from *The Scotsman* can be found at: (https://www.scotsman.com/news/people/scottish-maritime-museum-forced-by-vandals-to-stop-calling-ships-she-1-4913370).

A Really Inconvenient Truth: The article cited can be purchased from *Nature Geoscience*. However, an abstract of the article can be found at: (https://www.nature.com/articles/s41561-019-0329-3).

When Green is Actually Red: This is an opinion article abased on liberal support of the "Green New Deal." However, the essay does not reference any specific source.

Odds and Ends You Missed in the News: This article contains references from multiple sources including:

Swedish Government wants to ban ancient Viking symbols, claiming they "constitute incitement to hatred" at:

(https://voiceofeurope.com/2019/05/swedish-government-wants-to-ban-ancient-viking-symbols-claiming-they-constitute-incitement-to-hatred/).

John Cleese Suggests London Isn't 'Really an English City' at: (https://www.nytimes.com/2019/05/30/world/europe/john-cleese-london.html).

Spain's capitulation: Seville will have its first mosque in 700 years after the Reconquista at: (https://www.defendevropa.com/2019/news/islam/spains-capitulation-seville-will-have-its-first-mosque-in-700-years-after-the-reconquista/).

Poll: Only 18 Percent Of Germans Feel Free To Voice Views In Public at: (https://jonathanturley.org/2019/05/28/poll-on-18-percent-of-german-feel-free-to-voice-views-in-public/comment-page-1/).

France: As many practicing Muslims as Catholics among 18-29 year-olds at: (https://voiceofeurope.com/2019/05/france-as-many-practicing-muslims-as-catholics-among-18-29-year-olds/).

Go, Coach Joe!: The essay is an imaginary account of Joe Biden as a football coach. However, the reference to the "Chinese team" is from news accounts at the time in which Biden said that China is no competition for the United States.

Biden says China is 'not competition for us,' prompting pushback from both parties at: (https://www.washingtonpost.com/politics/biden-says-china-is-not-competition-for-us-prompting-pushback-from-republicans/2019/05/01/4ae4e738-6c68-11e9-a66d-a82d3f3d96d5_story.html).

Can Notre Dame Be Saved From Architects, Politicians, and Political Correctness?: Many news sources reported the proposed minaret for the restored *Notre Dame*. An article from *The Pluralist* can be found here: (https://pluralist.com/tom-wilkinson-notre-dame-minaret/).

Final Thoughts From A Conservative Vampire: Most references in this chapter come from general media sources.

An article about the Fox News poll, which shows strong support for impeachment, can be found at: (https://www.foxnews.com/politics/fox-news-poll-record-support-for-trump-impeachment).

The *Washington Examiner* article about young people and their support of socialism can be found at: (https://www.washingtonexaminer.com/opinion/high-number-of-young-people-are-willing-to-vote-for-a-socialist-like-alexandria-ocasio-cortez).

The nicknames "Pencil Neck" and "Pocahontas" have been referenced in previous chapters.